the Second Barrel

Other Books by Eric Sloane

A Reverence for Wood

A Sound of Bells

A Museum of Early American Tools

ABC Book of Early Americana

American Barns and Covered Bridges

American Yesterday

Book of Storms

Diary of an Early American Boy: Noah Blake—1805

Eric Sloane's Almanac

Eric Sloane's Weather Book

Folklore of American Weather

Look at the Sky

Our Vanishing Landscape

Return to Taos: A Sketchbook of Roadside Americana

The Seasons of America Past

An Age of Barns

Don't

The Cracker Barrel

Mr. Daniels and the Grange (with Edward Anthony)

The Second Barrel

by

ERIC SLOANE

Funk & Wagnalls
New York

Contents

Author's Note

The day after the first frost, when the old country store fired its potbellied stove, usually marked the beginning of winter. That was the time of year when screen doors were taken down and stacked away in a back room, chairs were taken in from the porch to be placed around the stove, and a new barrel of crackers appeared within arm's reach. The stage was set. Then along about early February, when city folks would think winter's back was broken and spring should appear over the horizon any minute, the farmer knew better. Farmers know that the winter season is exactly half over then, that the coldest time of the year occurs during the first week or two of February, and that the farmhouse woodpile should be just about half used up.

By February the pattern of country store conversation around the old stove usually grew thin and the free crackers were reduced to only a few broken pieces. Twice-told tales began to border on monotony and, as the old New England saying goes, folks would bring up tired stories "from the bottom of the barrel." But one of the pleasures of folk wit lies in its acceptance of (and even reverence for) repetition: like life itself, which consists of the same materials mixed up in so many different ways, the telling of tales may be likened to the art of serving the same soup, but spiced to please different tastes. And just when it seemed that all the stories of winter were done with, the potbellied stove was cleaned out and filled with fresh wood, the cuspidor had a scouring, a fresh barrel of crackers appeared, and the symphony of fresh opinion and time-worn country philosophy began all over again. "Some of the best stories of the year," as the saying goes, "come from the second barrel."

A few years ago when I started collecting cracker-barrel stories for a book, I worried about whether or not such a disconnected batch of yarns might be too rambling for the consistency an editor usually demands. But after *The Cracker Barrel* was published and I had received a startling number of compliments, comments, and expressions of hope for a further volume, I came to the conclusion that perhaps my season had not yet ended. It seemed to be February, and time for an encore. So take a seat at the potbellied stove while the boy tallies up your order, and help yourself to a few tidbits from. . . .

The Second Barrel

Eric Sloane
Warren Conn.

the
Second
Barrel

the Cracknell Barrel

Since I originally wrote *The Cracker Barrel,* I have been intrigued with the word "cracker," but then I've always been a bit crazy about semantics. The word "cracker" proved to be most interesting, for now and then it pops up in some new and different manner. For instance, I found an old store ledger which listed "crazy crackers." It didn't take long to learn that the word "crazy" first meant cracked or broken, as in the term "crazed" for cracked luster or glaze on porcelain. So the storekeeper's crazy crackers were simply broken crackers. There was also an old-time mill for breaking ore and grinding tin, called a "craze mill"; and sailors referred to a weak or cracked vessel as a "crazy boat."

In England they baked "biscuits" but in America they made "crackers." In fact there isn't a more American word than "cracker." Biscuit means "twice-cooked" or "baked," having evolved from the French word *bis* (twice) being added to *cuit* (cooked). The Germans had the same sort of word in *zwieback,* which comes from their *zwie* (twice) and *backen* (bake). But when the twice-baked bread reached our land it evolved into "cracker" because that was an all-American word. We "cracked jokes," shot off "firecrackers," said "by crackey," and we were often referred to in a rather uncomplimentary way as "American crackers." The earliest English dictionaries reveal that a cracker is "a loud and boisterous fellow."

My research took me back to a 1766 letter from Gavin Cochrane in America which defined the term to the Earl of Dartmouth in England: "I should explain to your Lordship," the letter reads, "what is meant by Crackers, a name they have got from being great boasters; they are a lawless set of rascals on the frontier of Virginia, Maryland, the Carolinas and Georgia." And that of course

[3]

is where the term "Georgia cracker" comes from! The same word was used by Shakespeare in describing a loud person: "What cracker is this same that deafs our ears with his abundance of superfluous breath?"

It was typical of an American to laugh at himself, and the show-off or loud fellow didn't always resent his nickname. In fact the fast talker and good salesman of the early 1800s was affectionately called a "crackerjack" and to be named a crackerjack was a red-white-and-blue compliment. "Wanted," reads an advertisement in a New York newspaper of 1845, "a crackerjack salesman."

Until Washington's time we were still eating biscuits and it wasn't until our early bakers began baking a particularly hard cake called a "cracknell" that the word "biscuit" disappeared from the American vocabulary. This American twice-baked bread was first made in 1792 by Theodore Pearson of Newburyport, Massachusetts. "Our soda-and-salt cracknells keep fresh many times more than common bread," his advertisement read. By 1860 the word "cracknell" had become "cracker," when, in the first large baking factory in Albany, New York, Belcher and Larrabee started competition against the smaller bakeries with its "B. and L. cracker." Soda crackers at that time were sold only by the barrel, often for use on ships and for shipment to the hill people of the South. As the hill people were already known as "crackers, living in crackerdom," they accepted baked soda crackers as their own idea and until the 1900s more crackers by the barrel were sold in Arkansas, Tennessee, and the Carolinas than anywhere else in the land. They still buy crackers there by the barrel (although it is now smaller and made of heavy cardboard), which may be why most people still believe the "Georgia cracker" got his name from eating crackers.

Barreling crackers started as an advertising scheme. The first big cracker companies placed a barrel of their wares for free sampling in New England country stores. But later the country storekeeper carried on the custom and soon a barrel of crackers was always to be found near the stove during the cold months. The cracker barrel had become part of the American scene.

Americana!

I venture to say that this is the first comment made about horns being historical. My collection of early American horns started as a New Year's Eve lark when I placed one at each guest's place at the table, but since then the shelf of old noisemakers has grown. Frequently, as my cleaning lady dusts them, they all topple over, domino-like.

"Good lands!" she says. "What in the world would anyone want with a shelf full of old tin horns?"

Some of my old horns are painted red, white, and blue for Independence Day or Election Day and some are green for Christmas or New Year's; others show traces of red and orange for Halloween fun. There just seemed to be something joyous about the toot or blast of a horn, and great-grandfather found a thousand such excuses for making himself known. At one time horns were even part of college equipment—they were used for cheering the team—but I've read old accounts of "horn sprees" at college parties that ended with a visit from the constable.

The fish peddler wasn't the only salesman with a horn; all itinerant peddlers had them. Their squawk as they announced their owner's arrival was likened to that of a hawk and that, believe it or not, is why peddlers were called "hawkers." The medicine man, the tinsmith, the scissors sharpener, the vegetable-and-meat man, all called their customers together with loud blasts on their tin horns.

If you are a collector of Winslow Homer's art, you may be familiar with his depiction of the old-time housewife calling her men in from the fields at noon with a dinner horn. The first household or farm horn was used for frightening Indians away or calling for help. I have one ancient household horn about four feet long that still sets my dog to howling and carries its sound farther than that of a bell or even a gunshot.

Everyone is familiar with the long slender brass or copper tallyho horn used by the old-time coachman to announce the arrival of his stage. A smaller version is still used in the South for signaling hunting dogs. But there is a tin horn that is even longer and thinner than the tallyho version; it has a larger mouthpiece. This was not really a horn at all but a "speaking tube" or "courting horn." In the early days, when everyone gathered around the hearth

[5]

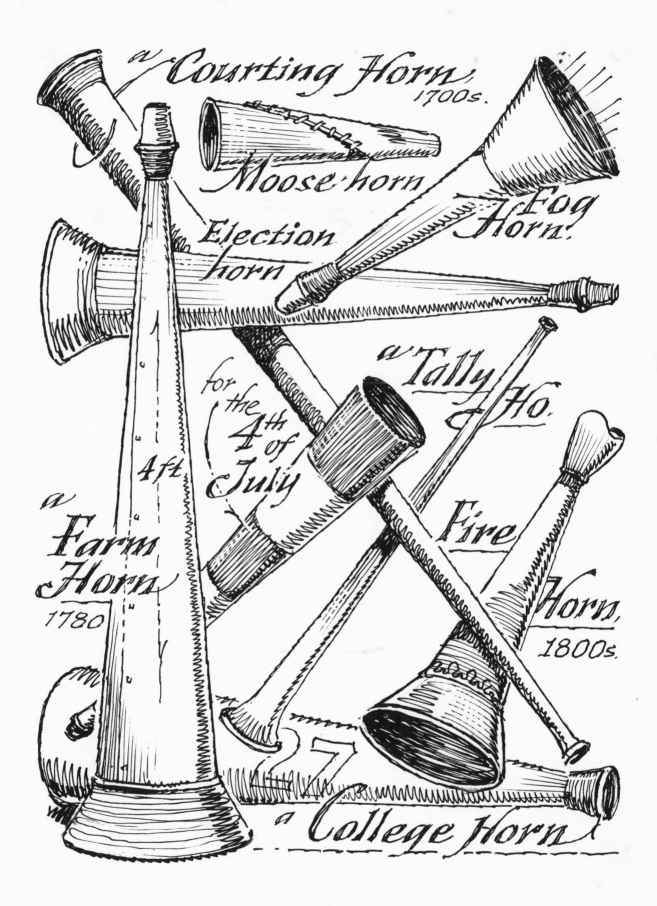

a Courting Horn, 1700s.

Moose horn

Election horn

Fog Horn.

a Tally Ho.

for the 4th of July

a Farm Horn 1780

4ft

Fire Horn, 1800s.

a College Horn

during the winter, the neighbor's boy usually came to visit the daughter, and their private conversations were reserved for youthful ears by this long whispering tube; the courting horn was not considered impolite. Sears, Roebuck's catalog as late as 1898 still carried a listing for both an "ear-horn" and a "whispering tube."

Perhaps you've wondered why the old-time firemen were posed carrying a silver horn; even now when the smoke-eaters parade, they carry a firehorn filled with flowers. And perhaps you've wondered why, in the sports pages, firemen teams are called "vamps." Well, the firehorn, which was used for shouting through instead of blowing through, was called a "vamping horn," because the first ones were made of leather and looked like the vamp or the upper part of a boot. There was still another horn that was blown to announce a fire and summon firemen, until bells took over that job during the early 1800s. Before bells were used for the purpose in American churches, the colonial minister summoned his congregation with a "church horn"; that sounds farfetched until we think of the religious ram's horn of the Jewish synagogue.

When I was a boy, most big city "candy stores" kept tin horns in stock, but if I were to try buying one now, I don't know where I would seek it. Even the Maine moose horn, the fisherman's horn, the foghorn, and the farm horn were homemade affairs, and the great tinsmith-made American horn has all but vanished from the scene. My shelf full of noisemakers, which must have caused quite a bit of jollity in their day, are only quiet antiques. My cleaning lady once picked up one that she'd toppled over and inquisitively gave it a toot. My dog howled and I came running to see what was up.

"It still works," she said. And we both laughed.

The Necessary

Up my way people talk funny. One neighbor has a "Rushing wolfhound" and lives in a "mid-Victorious house" with a brick "chimley." He came over to see my newly acquired farm and made note of the little building I've always called an outhouse.

"Nice 'nessy' you have there," he remarked. I had never heard it called that before. "We've *always* called them nessies," he told me. "They used to be called 'necessary houses'; some just called them 'necessaries.' But that was in the old days."

I found him to be correct, for according to my old dictionaries outhouses were formerly just outbuildings like smokehouses or springhouses or washhouses or wagonsheds; the privy (as my neighbor had said) was always referred to as the necessary house, or the necessary.

My necessary was an ancient abandoned structure that sat nicely and directly over a flowing stream, so the former owners didn't have much disposal trouble. They didn't, that is, until a few years before my time, when the neighbors got wind of it and complained. So the owners had to install indoor plumbing with a standard cesspool pipe running outside. Insistent folks they were, however, for I found that the pipe ran smack back into the brook and I had to dig a standard cesspool.

I called in a local expert, who admired my "sanitary system," crude as it was. "The brook don't go nowhere in particular," he said, "but I can still make you an incest pool if you think you need it. Styptic tanks are better, though."

He dug me a fine new cesspool and even he had to admire it. "That," he said reverently, "is a truly beautiful pool. It will be with you the rest of your life." He was wrong, of course.

The next day, however, when a big truck arrived with a bulldozer on it to start digging my pond, the bulldozer came in handy; it pulled the truck out of my nice new cesspool. "I'm sorry," the man said. "I've gone and busted through into your cyst pool."

Well, being a hopeless researcher, I went back to my old dictionaries to look up the word "cesspool," which wasn't there. After some thought, that proved natural, for there was no inside plumbing, either, when they were written; and so there were no accompanying cesspools. The word "cess" (also spelled "sess") referred to a personal land tax in the old days; from that came the words "assess" and "assessment." As far as I can figure, the first indoor plumbing was taxed by the number of connected drainage pools, which became known as "taxed pools," "cessed pools," or "cesspools." Well, my pool has certainly taxed *me* so far.

As a matter of fact, I've had cesspool troubles for years. The first incident was way back when I built my first house, and a hole suddenly appeared in the center of my lawn. So I phoned the contractor. "That's perfectly natural," he said. "Cesspools usually settle down like that. Just fill the hole with dirt."

But times were hard in those days and I wondered where I could find some free fill. Then, on my way to town one day I noticed road workers shoveling sand and debris from the road gutters. "Where do you throw that stuff?" I asked. "We haul it a few miles away," they told me, "and empty it into the dump." "Well, there's a much handier place right on my front lawn," I said. "And here's a five-dollar bill for your trouble." I thought I'd made a great bargain.

The hole got filled, but every time I left the house the pile of dirt continued to rise. There were also old bottles and cans and once even a dead cat, and pieces of an old corset, a bicycle tire. When the pile had reached about six feet high, I stayed home to lie in wait for the road workers, to stop them.

Yes, I've had cesspool trouble for years.

The First MUFF c.1700

Today's fashions, according to the designers, are making men "brave and unafraid of change." Indeed, some of the men I've seen must be pretty brave just to face themselves in the mirror, and to risk unsolicited remarks. Clothing hitherto suitable only for fancy dress balls or for burlesque comics is suddenly fashionable for men. I guess the appropriate Halloween costume will eventually be a gray flannel suit with collar and tie.

I despise men who look like women and I am reluctant to talk about women who try to look like men. Notice that I am more lenient about women; besides, women have been copying us men for a long while, but for men who believe they should have any of the charms of womanhood—words always fail me. I am reminded of a shopgirl I saw in a subway, who was beholding, mouth open in amazement, two womanish fags carry on across the aisle. As she shook her head in disbelief, her eyes met mine. "Sort of makes you want to vomit, doesn't it?" she said. Looking at their clothes I, too, agreed.

Clothing's function, it seems, should be primarily utilitarian, its main use for keeping the body warm. Abraham Lincoln wore a shawl, but he wasn't imitating women. In fact, I'd like to revive the idea of shawls for men because they are warm and comforting as well as becoming. Consider the male swimmer who throws a big bath towel over his shoulders after a strenuous swim, or the football player who sits out his turn with a blanket around his shoulders.

As I write these words in my barn studio, I have a small lap robe over my shoulders and I don't feel a bit sissy; I merely feel warm and comfortable.

[11]

Remember muffs? My mother had a big muff with mink tails hanging from it, and inside a compartment for ladies' trivia. Now it would be lipstick and cigarettes and matches, but my mother kept Sen-Sen, a nest of fancy handkerchiefs, and smelling salts in her muff. I'll bet there aren't many who even remember smelling salts, when women were always swooning and ammonia salts were supposed to bring them back to proper consciousness. Now they say that the fainting habit was caused by tight corsets, but I don't believe it. The word "faint" is a doublet for "feint" (to pretend), and when a woman fainted in the old days, most likely she was just being Victorian. That was when ladies didn't always have their own way as they do now, and fainting (or feigning) was just a part of being a woman.

I don't expect you to believe it, but the first muffs in America were worn by men. Originally they carried their inks and coffee-break ingredients or whatever else they needed from the house to their place of business in the confines of a small fur robe; later the little robe was stitched together into a roll, and I have found several eighteenth-century references to a "man's bearskin muff."

Although long hair and necklaces have now invaded man's world, I have often wondered why men don't carry handbags, too. But then I realized that we certainly do carry handbags. We call them "attaché cases." If you think all those Madison Avenue leather cases contain only contracts, be informed that you'll often find them containing cigars, vitamins, address books, a clean shirt, perhaps shaving equipment, and often a bottle. Men used to look a lot fatter when they carried everything in their pockets than they do now. The watch pocket in men's trousers has already vanished, the side pockets are no longer built king-sized, and the rear pocket for carrying a wallet is no longer fashionable. One interesting thing about those tight leotard-type pants that some men wear is that there isn't room for pockets. Now that most men have ditched the vest, they can no longer carry objects in all those pockets, and the watch has gone from a pocket to the wrist. Now, according to news reports, all odds and ends are being carried in a "Madison Avenue handbag." It makes sense.

Recently I spent some time on jury duty and I made a game of trying to analyze people. Nearly all the guilty guys kept their hands in their pockets. There they were, the accused and delinquent, each approaching the bench with their hands in their pockets. If you ever serve on a jury, that's how you can tell the good guys from the bad guys. Lawyers have often been accused of having their hands in a client's pocket, but you'll never see one with his hands in his *own* pockets.

1853

They don't make them like that any more!

If I could remember how many sleds I've had in my life, they would most likely number over a dozen. Yet I have no idea where they have gone. Flexible Flyers they were, made of the best steel and polished oak. Yet I have one tiny sled, all handmade in 1853, which I shall never part with. I'm certain it has reached such a stage of antiquity that it should never be cast away.

Our ways are strange indeed.

A vanishing American trait is the reverence we once had for our vehicles. A sled or a child's wagon used to be kept in prime condition and passed on to be used from generation to generation. When ancient barns are torn down now, there are always family sleighs and farm wagons still in excellent working condition found stored away from the weather, close to the rafters. Their wheels or runners, mostly wooden, are far more delicate than those on today's vehicles. Perhaps, in times past, we used to appreciate the work that vehicles did or the good times they afforded, and thereby evolved a gratefulness for them.

I recall as a child wiping and oiling my scooter, then later on, caring for my bicycle. I seldom finished with it for the day without oiling it and wiping it off. When I had my first automobile (a Chevrolet Baby Grand), I kept even its running boards clean and waxed. The underside of the mudguards, where mud splashed, was painted a bright red and I kept that clean too. Now I ponder about bicycles left lying on the lawns of my neighbors, even overnight in the rain.

All this came to mind when my dog Spook scratched at the house door to be let out. When he went out, he scratched at the car door to be let in. He is an old dog and has become strangely attached to the comfort and importance of what I'm sure he regards as a big doghouse on wheels. He has a deep sentiment for the confines of the back seat of the car, and as I have sat about a quarter of a century in front seats, I think I know what he feels.

I once had a friend who courted a girl in the back seat of his Lincoln Continental. Years later after they were married and the car was ready to be either junked or sold, he couldn't bear to part with the big leather cushion which had become so important a part of his life. So he sold the car sans back seat: by adding legs to the cushions, he has made a comfortable and most meaningful fireside seat. I think I know what he means too.

When you stop to think about how many hours we use up sitting in automobiles, some of us would find that about half our lives are spent there. When we realize how the automobile serves us in all seasons, often in tense or urgent situations, speeding us to rescues, to hospitals, or bearing us to funerals, to our work, our shopping, or our pleasure, I don't wonder that anyone (or even my dog Spook) might read personality into a vehicle and thereby form a strange attachment.

I do wonder, though, about the new disregard for machinery. The last time I motored to the city I counted twenty-two automobile hulks sitting on the roadside, stripped of their wheels. People who tire of their cars, it seems, can remove their registration plates and just walk away without any worry of receiving some kind of penalty. The only known law they break is that concerning illegal parking, but as most cars have had several owners, the cost of tracing the most recent owner would far exceed any fine attached. It even costs the city about twenty-five dollars to remove each abandoned car, and there are fifty thousand occurrences each year in New York alone. Nationally, car abandonment has reached an expense of over ten million dollars yearly.

When he went to England on a vacation recently, one fellow bought an inexpensive little car and, being in a great hurry (and American), he motored to the ship's pier and abandoned the car when he boarded the boat to return home. The worth of the car, he had decided, was too small for the time-consuming trouble of trying to sell it. Two months later, when he received a special letter from Scotland Yard, his heart trembled. "My dear sir," it read. "Your vehicle was found abandoned and therefore it was auctioned to the highest bidder. The cost of hauling it has been deducted, and you will find the balance enclosed in form of a money order."

I hope there will always be an England!

Home is where the Hearth is

I'll bet I'm the only one who thinks that a fireplace tells something about the character of its owner. I recall how the author Van Wyck Brooks saved the ashes and carefully patted them into a flattened pyramid in the fireplace, with the same meticulousness as he fashioned his stories. On the other hand, Norman Mailer builds a spectacular fire and scatters the ashes carelessly into the room, while Arthur Miller plans his fire like a complicated stage play, even starting his cooking charcoal first in a little section of stovepipe. I have friends who make fancy paper fans to put between andirons during the summer and some who use pots of flowers. There are those sad people who think a fireplace is for warming a room instead of the soul; they often tolerate it as a decoration, putting in it clean birch logs that are never to be burned. I have one conservationist friend who saves all his newspapers to roll and tie into tight logs of newsprint, which burn remarkably well; another, a scientist, is particular about using the proper wood for kindling, selecting a soft wood for beginning the fire and finding only the hardest wood suited for banking a lasting fire.

The connoisseur knows that a cord of hickory will give as much heat as two cords of maple, and as much as four cords of pine. But only a novice would burn pine logs for heat instead of splitting them for kindling. I've found the

American Indians of the Southwest are experts at fireplace lore, mixing up a kindling paste from ashes and kerosene; their use of piñon wood as incense creates an almost hypnotic effect. Usually the women design the Indian fireplaces, which are often built in the corner of the room; I've never seen one that didn't burn perfectly. Indians will be quick to regard fireplace craft as a reflection of one's personality.

While cleaning my own living-room hearth after last night's party, my thoughts raced back to Vera Whitehouse and the time I lit my cigarette and threw the burned match into her fireplace. Vera was as old school as they came, and when she tapped her gold-headed cane against the marble Newport mantel, an exceedingly proper butler appeared. "Thank you, Rogers," she said. "Will you kindly remove the match Mr. Sloane threw into the fireplace? You probably neglected to place the ash trays properly."

At the time I felt somewhat offended, but Vera did things like that. "My fireplace," she later explained, "is the heart of my living room; I cannot bear to have it used as a garbage disposal or even as an ash tray." Now after half a century and some few dozen fireplaces of my own, I know how she felt about her hearth, for mine is still scattered with cigarette butts, candy wrappers, and other trivia from last night's party. I remember that in times past most of these things burned, but modern filter tips and foil cigarette packs seem never to disappear.

My hearth (Vera would be proud to know if she were still alive) is the heart of my living room, and I always think of the word "hearth" as it once was used—an ancient pronunciation of the word "heart." Nowadays the television set is the heart of most homes and I suppose the time will arrive when fireplaces become obsolete curiosities.

The hearth was once a courting place; it was also where the family gathered for serious talks or for holiday fun. Outdoor sounds have a strange way of becoming amplified and hollow-sounding, as if from another world, as they tumble down the big old chimneys. There was something about the inner snugness of a fireplace that gave a feeling of import, of security, and of reverence for the home. Even after the flames had died down, there were still lively embers glowing throughout the night to stir dreams of the past and hopes for the future. There was something comforting, too, in knowing that your father and his father had thought "fireplace thoughts."

Now, when the TV set has replaced the hearthplace, we gather to witness confusion, revolt, and violence. When it is turned off, the magic of electronics explodes into a dull silence and there is nothing left but a plastic box with a big blind eye.

That is when I leave the TV corner and stretch out in front of my fireplace to enjoy the lost art of thinking—and I give thanks that I live in an age in which there are still fireplaces.

I Remember Hatracks.

Most of the commonplace things of my younger days have now become antiques, it seems. Recently I decided to acquire a roll-top desk and a hatrack.

"We have a quaint hatrack for three hundred dollars," they told me at a local antique shop. "Hatracks are obsolete now, and hard to come by." I thought you could still buy them at any furniture store but as few people wear hats any more, I guess the hatrack, like the roll-top desk, has joined vanishing Americana.

I still feel unconventional because I do not wear a hat, but when I see some men waiting in long lines to "buy their hats back" from a hatcheck girl, I feel better. Some fellows pay an average of two hundred dollars a year just to get their own hats back. I've seen Jim Farley, Harry Hershfield, Lowell Thomas, Rube Goldberg, and about twenty other notables in line at once at my luncheon club, wasting what must have been a few thousand dollars' worth of top manpower time for silly hats they really didn't need.

I remember during Prohibition days when everyone wore hats. Some night clubs then depended on obtaining the fifty-thousand-dollar advance from a hatcheck concession group before they could afford to open. Sometimes the club went broke but the hatcheck concession always came out on top. The custom of tipping for checking your hat goes back to about 1800. Before that, the "tip" was paid in advance, for quicker service in the old coffeehouses. There was a box for this purpose marked "To Insure Promptness," which was later abbreviated to T.I.P. or tip.

There are a lot of other complications connected with hat wearing; such as wondering if it is really worth the trouble of chasing your hat down the avenue when it blows off, and what to do with your hat in an elevator. In an office-building elevator I seldom remove my hat for ladies but in a hotel I always do. In Gimbels store and in Macy's in New York City, I don't remove my hat, but in the fashionable Abercrombie and Fitch you'll be frowned upon if you forget to do so. I did notice, though, that Macy's elevator operator always called out "up" and "down," while at Abercrombie and Fitch they say "ascending" and "descending," so maybe there is some strange aesthetic difference.

Often a man will walk through the lobby or along the halls of a hotel with a lady without removing his hat; yet there is something cloistered, even ecclesiastical, about the mood of an elevator. Thus, the sight of an elevator door opening and revealing a group of saintly men holding their hats there, in the dimlit niche, in reverence to womanhood, is completely moving to the soul of the observer.

One elevator, I recall, was filled with hatted men and one Negro woman. When a young Western Union messenger boy entered and immediately removed his cap, about ten men instantly were shamed into doing the same. But then the messenger took some papers from inside his hat and replaced it upon his head, leaving an elevator full of chagrined men.

Another crowded elevator was entered by a small man carrying large packages in both hands, followed by a large and commanding wife. This lady, who seemed to know the lore and etiquette of elevators, immediately reached over and removed her husband's hat and held it till the group descended to the ground floor, then placed the hat back on the obedient little man's head. Oddly enough, she had been the only woman passenger.

Though I seldom wear hats, I own several. Recently, while packing an armful of my things into a trunk to be moved to a new studio, I put two hats on my head, one atop the other. Without realizing it, I continued to the city wearing both hats at the same time. Strangely enough, I made several business stops and nobody seemed to be alarmed. It wasn't till I checked my coat and hat (or rather "hats") that I learned my mistake. The checkroom lady gave me two checks instead of one. "One check will do," I said. "They are both mine." Later I called for my double headgear, put it on, and walked through the lobby unashamed. After all, when fashion allows women to appear as if they had forgotten their skirts and men may wear fancy dress costumes with long hair and necklaces, what's so wrong with two hats instead of one? I'm an extremist, too.

Sex and the Button

It is interesting how one thing leads to another; like the time someone wrote to me and asked if I knew why men's buttons are always sewn on the right side and women's buttons on the left. It still doesn't seem very important, but I am one who wakes up in the middle of the night with some silly word on his mind, gets up, and heads for the dictionary. I used to sleep in the library, but now I keep the dictionary by my bed. Anyway, the "left and right" in connection with men and women led to a one-man study of some remarkable phenomena.

For example, I observed that most men stir liquids counterclockwise while women stir in the opposite manner. Men put their coats on hangers on a closet pole so that the coat faces the left. Even when a hanger is curved to fit the opposite position, a man will often hang his coat incorrectly on it, always facing left. A woman scratches her matches outward or away from herself while a man scratches inward and toward himself. You will know that a man inserted the roll of toilet paper if the hanging portion falls outward, into the room; a woman invariably lets the loose end hang against the wall. Ask a woman to look at her fingernails and she will hold her open hand at arm's length; a man will clench his fist and inspect his nails "upside down."

I notice, too, that women tend to sit opposite one another so that they can look directly into the face of their companion, while a man would rather sit *beside* his friend. You will see a group of men at any bar, all looking straight ahead at the bottles behind the bar instead of at their companions and talking out of the sides of their mouths. Ask a man the color of another man's eyes and he will seldom know; ask a woman about eyes, male or female, and she will probably tell you at once.

The problem of why women's buttons are on the left and men's on the right, however, ran me into a maze of legendary solutions involving swords and pistols with men and convenience for nursing mothers with women. But the costume department of the Metropolitan Museum of Art agrees with me that these are all dubious and far-fetched explanations. And, as they seemed stumped for a correct solution, I feel free to spout my own findings. Like those of most other lecherous males, my ideas are apt to be Freudian.

It involves why men usually push their thread through a captive needle hole (rather like the sex act) while a woman generally will hold her thread in one hand and push the hole of her needle *over* the thread. In the same manner a man will push an object into place while a woman will passively try to pull it into place.

After poring through my collection of ancient portraits, I found that men used to have enormous coat buttons while women's buttons were very tiny. Possibly the true answer to the button problem might be that women used buttonhooks. Men must have used the right hand to *push* their right coat buttons through the left buttonholes, while women must have used their right hands to operate a buttonhook, *pulling* the left-hand button through in a truly feminine manner. Sex again!

Anyway, just to make sure I hadn't left any stones unturned, I called my friend Norton Mockridge. "Hi, Norton," I began, "I have a funny question to ask you. It's about how men do certain things one way and women do the same things in another fashion."

But before I could explain further, Norton quipped: "Yeah. Great, isn't it?"

the Wyeth and wherefore

Maybe you've wondered why so many antique objects were signed and dated. On boxes and tools, blankets and samplers, even in the brickwork of old houses or on the slate roofs of some New England barns you will find the names of the makers or builders set down. At first you get the idea that folks were pretty self-centered, or just looking for publicity, or wanting to be remembered. The fact is that the pre–Civil War era was an age of original works. You never heard of an artist doing a painting without signing his name, did you?

Just about everything made in the early days was an original work. The signature didn't make it worth more to anyone but the maker. Nowadays there are few original works because nearly everything has been factory-made for us; therefore the value of an original work has skyrocketed. And the *signed* original is something special, indeed.

I own an original Andrew Wyeth picture. How about that? Sometimes when I want to enjoy the richness of my lofty position in life, I put on my plum-colored smoking jacket, sit where I can get a good view of my Wyeth, and sip my sherry. Actually I could not afford even his recently published big book of pictures. And it is true that my original Wyeth is very small. In fact, if you must know, it is only a sketch that he added to his signature when he wrote me a letter. I just folded over the letter and framed the sketch and signature where Wyeth had explained to me the proportions of his millhouse. But owning even that is pretty good for a local boy like me.

I've been offered remarkable amounts for my Wyeth sketch and of course I wouldn't sell it; but I can't help wishing my signature was worth that much. The trick, of course, is to keep it rare. George Washington went all over the country and signed his name lots of times, but Wyeth is more careful and I guess his signature brings a better price. George could have learned a lot from Andrew.

Let me tell you why a Sloane signature, for example, isn't worth very much. Being a timid author who always wants to please his readers with a little something extra, I started adding a sketch to my signatures a long while ago. Now people think the sketch is part of my name, and even the bank gives me trouble when I sign only my name to a check. People think that every Sloane book they buy should have a Sloane signature and sketch; some have asked me to add things like: "To my old pal Mortimer on his sixteenth birthday. Keep up the good work in your painting, Mort. From your fellow artist, Eric Sloane." I wonder what Mortimer (whoever he is) will think about that inscription? I'll bet he hasn't even read a Sloane book—but maybe he has framed the decorated autograph.

Nowadays a Sloane book isn't worth a hoot without the signature sketch, and it's getting so bad that in time I guess you may get your money refunded if the book hasn't one. But the whole deal gives me a great idea for all authors: I'll bet Norman Mailer, for example, could sell more books with a fancy autograph on the flyleaf with some of his nice four-letter words added. Or any author could charge a dollar or so for each signature, which would usually be more than his royalty for the book. This might open up a brand-new field to writers, who could then concentrate more on inscribing autographs than on writing the contents of their books.

And so I'm thinking about opening up a "Famous Writer's Autographing School." By mail I could teach you to do appropriate sketches, incorporating the recipient's hobbies, or to do Christmas, birthday, or Bar Mitzvah gift books, to make a plain everyday book a rare collector's item.

After all, anyone can write a *book*. Don't we all?

POLL →

HELVE

← BIT - - >

the all-American Axe

Perhaps the tool least regarded in America is the axe. Everyone has an axe lying around somewhere, but few axes have the same care lavished on them that is afforded other tools; almost none has the cutting edge that it deserves. You'll seldom find a man who will think twice before lending his axe. To find it he'll have to look in a dark corner of the cellar, or it may be clunked into a chopping block where it was left out in the weather. Yet a century ago the axe was the most important implement in America. There were manufacturers who made nothing but axes. There was a choice of some fifty designs, and every man had his favorite. He knew his axe handle length better than he knew his own shirt sleeve measurements.

You could once tell a man's character to some degree by his axe. Uniquely a man's own, like his signature, his axe handle design was often kept in the form of a blank pattern from which to fashion future handmade helves, as axe handles were formerly called. A man might season some special chunk of hickory by the fireplace all winter long, to prepare it for carving an axe helve in the spring.

The early axehead wasn't just one piece of metal; it had a "bit" of special steel hammered into the cutting edge, as shown in the sketch above. Any experienced woodsman knew that axe bits chipped easily when they were very cold, so he heated the axehead and blade before using it in winter weather. A book could be written just on American axe lore for, with this single implement, the pioneer went into the forest and cleared the land; with it he split firewood, built a cabin, made furniture, and on occasion even used it for protection against marauding animals and Indians. But not many would read such a book, for few of us truly appreciate axes nowadays.

I always thought that to be a proper countryman, you had to start with a good axe, so when I first moved from the city, I stopped in at Abercrombie and

Fitch's shop in New York to buy one. They hadn't had any calls for axes lately, it seemed, and outside of a folding axe and a mountain climber's implement, the only other one they could find turned up in an old catalog. After some searching they found this item in one of the storerooms. "Don't bother to wrap it," I said. "My train leaves in ten minutes and I have just enough time if I run for it." Luckily I knew the house detective, but even then he seemed startled at seeing me dashing out into New York's Madison Avenue with an axe. The conductor on the train, however, didn't know me. Probably there isn't a law forbidding passengers carrying axes; at any rate, he merely shook his head either in wonder or disbelief.

When I arrived home, I found that my nice new axe had a split in the handle. It certainly had to be returned, and this time I decided to wrap it. The same conductor stopped in his tracks when he recognized the telltale shape. He greeted me warily. "Hello again. You've wrapped it this time."

In New York, the store manager apologized and I was soon on my way to the country again with another axe in its axe-shaped wrapping. The conductor had become accustomed to me now. "How is your axe?" he asked. "Fine, thank you," I said.

But would you believe it? The store had given me a short-handled axe, not at all suited to my arm length. You can guess the rest. I became known as the commuter who carries an axe, and I didn't make many friends in the club car, even after I had obtained a proper implement and stopped toting axes.

The Vanishing Art of Penmanship

I have just received a nice letter from Mr. Skyzchksgexb. At least that is what his signature looks like to me. I guess if I sent it to a handwriting expert he might tell me the writer was a most distinguished person. I'd say, distinguished as he may be, he is careless and rude, and if he has no more self-respect than to scribble his own name in an unintelligible manner, he might better sign with an X.

F. Scott Fitzgerald said, "You don't write because you want to say something: you write because you've got something to say. And if you have something to say, mumbling by mouth or by pen is just bad taste."

The handwriting of the Pilgrim and Puritan fathers was generally poor; but by the 1700s penmanship had become an American project. Old school contracts often refer to teachers as "writing masters" and a chief requisite of the colonial teacher was that he be a good teacher of penmanship. Reading, 'Riting and 'Rithmetic, in that order, was what schools taught.

Writing masters were honored in every community during the 1700s and adults as well as children took lessons from them. Abiah Holbrook of Boston was one of the better-known writing masters: one of his scholars created so individual a signature that his name even now is linked with the writing of a signature. It was John Hancock, of course.

It seems odd that the exquisitely fine and readable writing of the early days was done with crude goose quills. The writing master made and repaired the school pens, which often was a two-hour chore before class time. Boys were never allowed to make their own pens until they were twelve, at which magic age they were presented with penknives. For some reason we still call pocket knives that.

"Demonstrations" of handwriting were as popular in the old days as demonstrations of sewing (as seen in samplers), and many school notebooks have pages of finely drawn alphabets. Even the first pages of schoolbooks were devoted to well-written rhymes such as:

[25]

Blunderbuss a s gun 5.
Blun derbuss ash short
Blun der buss ash ort gun
Blun derbuss ashort
Blunderbuss ashor
Blunderbuss ashor
Blunderbuss ashort
Blunderbuss ashor
Blunderbuss asho

Henry Dedrick May 24th 1814

Steal not this book, for if you do
The Devil will be after you.

or

When land is gone and money spent,
Then learning is most excellent.

If this you see, Remember me.

Letters from school nowadays are all too often requests for money, poorly scribbled or typewritten. But at one time they were sincere exhibitions of what had been learned and gracious expressions of gratitude for having been afforded that learning. I have collected these old letters and regret that such things do not exist today: not only penmanship has changed, but also the human mind. If you don't believe this, let me show you a letter written from school by John Quincy Adams when he was nine years old, to his father:

Braintree, June the 2nd, 1777.

Dear sir: I love to receive letters very well, much better than I love to write them. I make a poor figure at composition, my head is too fickle, my thoughts are running after bird's eggs, play, and trifles till I get vexed with myself. I have but just entered the 3rd volume of Smollett 'tho I had designed to have got it half through by this time. I have determined this week to be more diligent. . . . I have set myself a stent and determine to read the 3rd volume half out. If I can but keep my resolution, I will write again at the end of the week and give a better account of myself. I wish, Sir, you would give me some instructions with regard to my time and advise me how to proportion my studies and my play, in writing; I will keep them by me and endeavor to follow them. I am, dear Sir, with a present determination of growing better, yours.

JOHN QUINCY ADAMS

P.S. Sir, if you will be so good as to favour me with a blank-book, I will transcribe the most remarkable occurrences I meet with my reading which will serve to fix them upon my mind.

And the pre-Spencerian penmanship would have warmed the cockles of the heart of P. R. Spencer, the creator of this style of writing. He died in 1864, and since that time, incidentally, the American handwriting has done everything except improve.

A Statue for the Park

Everywhere you go in America, you'll see statues of pioneer men and soldiers. Those Civil War statues of fellows who shot their brothers, for instance, with lists below of those who lost their lives in the "glory" of war, are remembered each Memorial Day with wreaths and flowers. But what about women? The women who pioneered America were a lot more important than most people think. They looked prettier, too.

Pioneer man has left a trail of monuments to remind us of his resourcefulness and craftsmanship, but pioneer woman has so far been sadly neglected. Although the men's creations—the farmhouses and bridges and stone walls and orchards—still live on, except for a few patchwork quilts and hooked rugs, what women did is apt to slip our minds.

We have a few schoolbook heroines like Barbara Frietchie and Mollie Pitcher, but the real story is that of the women who just tended garden, did the cooking, carded the wool from the sheep, spun it, and wove the cloth to make clothing and blankets for all the family; who canned the fruits and vegetables, made the lye and then the soap, made the candles, tended the chickens and plucked the geese for mattress and pillow stuffings, milked the cows and cleaned the barn as well as the house; who also hauled all the water, and fashioned the baskets and boxes for cookies and pies, ground the corn for baking the bread, peeled all the apples for making the apple butter and cider, and in between chores found time to bear an army-sized family and to teach them while clothing and feeding them.

Now, as we regard the back-breaking chore of being a pioneer woman, we immediately pity her. But any psychologist will tell you that for centuries the prime joy of womanhood has been her awareness of being useful, and that the national sickness of women today lies in their feeling useless. Actually man has a touch of the same *maladie du jour* because everything is now done for us and we are robbed of the pleasure of making or creating, even finding out things for ourselves.

The fops and aristocrats of yesterday chose their wives as they might choose their waistcoats, but the farmer's wife knew she was a part of the farm equipment and she enjoyed being that important. Secretly, I'll bet, she knew she was more important than her husband.

The golden age of farming is about done with, so the pretty housewife of today can breathe a sigh of relief. Only a few cases come to mind, like an ad I saw recently in an Ozark newspaper:

Farmer forty years old seeks woman about the same age with serviceable tractor: object matrimony. Send photo of tractor.

I recall a scene in *I Remember Mama* in which Mama, waiting a doctor's report on her child, found a scrub pail and started scrubbing the hospital waiting room floor to relieve her nervous tension. More recently I heard that an abandoned mother of six, finding herself without rent money, baked pies and cakes all day Friday. On Saturday morning she set up a little table on the town green. By noon she had sold everything and had enough to pay the rent and a bit left over toward next month's rent, too.

If you study the old tintypes, you will notice the man always sits and the woman stands. She usually has her hand on the man's shoulder as if to comfort him. Perhaps the man did the most sitting and, anyway, that was his stock position in pictures. Most times he looked pretty silly in those pictures, with a lot of whiskers and a stovepipe hat on his head; but those women were subjects for any sculptor. They had a world of character in their faces, and their hands were as strong as they were gentle. The only famous pioneer man I knew of who didn't have a woman doing most of his work was Johnny Appleseed, and he went around with a tin pot on his head, according to the legend.

American Table Language

Being a man of plain tastes, the mumbo-jumbo of fancy menu language has always bored me, yet I am intrigued by the derivation of food words. Sirloin, for instance. I understand that an English monarch, when confronted with a specially fine cut of meat, drew his sword and dubbed it "Sir Loin." I am amused by the fact that the avocado is a mispronunciation of the Mexican word *ahuacatl,* which really meant testicle. The old Aztec pronunciation was too hard for the Spanish, who slurred it to sound like their word for lawyer or "advocate" (*abogado* or *aguacate*). I like knowing that both hash and hatchet come from the French word "to chop."

Many years ago and once upon my time, I sat with a restaurant man named Charles Feltman, in Coney Island. "Coney Island" he told me, "was named after the rabbits they used to shoot here in the early days; coney was the Dutch name for rabbit (*konijn*). Folks once kidded me about the frankfurters at my restaurant, saying they were made from rabbit meat; 'hot rabbit-furters' they called them. But that was a long time ago. Now they call them 'hot dogs' and not many people realize that serving them on rolls was my invention.

"We Americans were always pretty inventive in the kitchen," he told me. "Even chop suey was our own idea." Then he went on to relate how an Italian dishwasher in San Francisco took over a Chinese restaurant when the owner died. He was a very good cook, but he mixed all the leftovers in a big bowl and served it as a house specialty. "Phooey!" cried one of his Chinese customers. "That is just a lot of *tsa-sui*" (which means old odds-and-ends in their language). A fight resulted, which ended up being reported on the front pages of a San Francisco newspaper, and was followed by a lawsuit. "Chopped sewage was not a nice thing for him to call my food," said the restaurant owner. But the name "chop suey" stuck and Chinese restaurants have ever since been serving the mixed dish and calling it that, giving us what they think we want. And sure enough, we seem to want it.

The romance of American eating habits would fill an interesting book and

The First Fork

1600

1630

Pipkin.
(sauce boiler)
c. 1680

Sneaker.
(punch-cup)

CLAY
Twiffler
(pudding dish)
1750

Trencher
(INDIVIDUAL
WOODEN CUTTING
board

Forked-spoons
1730

Porringer

(WOOD)

I've been collecting notes on them for years. Take the origin of the common table fork. We ate with our fingers and a knife and a spoon until the fork (which really had started in Italy) was brought to America by Governor Winthrop of Massachusetts. It was brought to the table in a leather case, and the Puritans denounced it as "crude and devilish." Actually the first forks were just split or "forked" knives but later they developed into very sharp two-tined instruments. The present day three- and four-tined fork came along in the 1800s.

When the main course was done in the eighteenth century, a basket called a voyder (or voider) was passed around to collect the trencher, knife, crumbs, and whatever was left over. The trencher was not a giant pewter plate as the antique dealers might have you believe; it was a little slab of wood (like an individual cutting board) used for serving and slicing meat.

Then there were names now forgotten, like the "twiffler," a dish for puddings; the "table-pot" for ale; and the "sneaker," a container for punch. You "divided" or "portioned" a roast, "spoiled" or "thrusted" a chicken, "broke" a goose, "halved" a shore bird, and "pierced" a turkey. The table napkin was like a small tablecloth that completely filled the lap, or could be tied around the neck like a reversed cape.

In Washington's day, you *breakfasted, dined,* and *supped.* The midday meal was always dinner—an evening meal was never called that. Going home after a meal was usually a long trip and the roads were not safe at night, so special meals were never served in the evening. Instead, for formal functions, meals for special guests or party occasions were held at noon and called dinners. When the day was over, eating was an informal affair partaken of sometimes in nightdress, often just tea, coffee, soup, or wine to be supped; and that was called supper. Supper was seldom taken at table, but more often from the lap while sitting near the fireplace.

At least there was something gracious about eating in the old days that is missing in these times of eateries and pizza palaces, diners and luncheonettes. If you really must know (and I think you should), the word "lunch" means a "lump of food" and a "luncheon," according to my old dictionaries, is "as much food as can be held in one hand."

He who writes for a living is automatically in the word business, and I find the study and research of words a fascinating hobby. Some folks are thrilled by making a hole in one on the golf course, but I get that much satisfaction every time I make some rare semantic find. Like when I solved the riddle of how the expression "dead as a doornail" started. That was when an old-time carpenter reminded me to "deaden the nail" which I'd hammered through a board instead of telling me to "clinch" it. Ancient doors were made from vertical boards on the outside and horizontal boards on the inside fastened together with handwrought nails that, when struck through, had to be hammered flat. This, I finally learned, was called "deadening" a doornail, for all old-time doornails had to be "dead."

Another find was the origin of "johnnycake." A little flat wooden board used by Kit Carson was referred to in his diary as his "journeycake board." Even then he was using a word already obsolete, for in 1805 in Parkinson's *Tour,* it was said

> . . . the lower class of people mix the flour into a paste and lay it before the fire on a board or shingle . . . this is called a Johnny cake.

For years I had been intrigued by contemplating the habit of small boys stretching out the left forefinger and running the right finger along it in a slicing motion as they called, "Shame on you." Then I found an ancient print that gave me the answer. It seems that when the old word "fie" was commonly used to indicate "shame upon you," people also had hand signs similar to the present-day "thumbs down," "V for victory," etc. The shout of "Fie!" also indicated to an actor he had displeased the audience: but by raising the hands and crossing the fingers, the message was the same. By using one index finger actually to point toward the actor and "sawing" with the other, an even more accusing emphasis was displayed. And that is how youngsters came to make that motion with their index fingers while singing, "Shame, shame, everybody knows your name!"

Our common exclamation "Gee!" is, of course, short for—or at least considered more decent than—"God!" Egad was Anglo-Saxon for "By God!" and the archaic word "zounds" originally began as "God's wounds!" A tough one to pin down was "balderdash!" but an early dictionary defines it as a barber's mixture of soapsuds and cologne. In the 1770s, when whiskey or wine was badly mixed or adulterated, they referred to it as tasting like soapsuds or balderdash; finally it became a general expression meaning nonsense.

When I stub my toe it seems natural to say "Ouch!" Yet strangely enough this occurs only in the English language. Sometime in the 1300s in England, when a wild boar dug his tusk into a hunter, he "delivered an owche, or a blow by the tusk." Thus, later on, when people were hurt they considered themselves "owched."

The word "hello" began as "halloo," which was "a cry to excite dogs, shouted in imitation of a hunting hound." It was never used as a greeting, believe it or not, until less than a century ago; it is a word which began with the telephone. Experimenters first shouted the "hunting dog cry" over the first "telegraph-phone," then it was lessened into a calm "halloo," and finally it became the official telephone greeting "hello." The first printed use of hello, as far as I could discover, was in 1885. That might sound like a lot of balderdash to you, but zounds and egad, it is so!

Those wiggly signs above are on my typwriter and are used by everyone every day; yet would you believe it, there aren't many people who know what they are called. Of course this is an abbreviation sign for "and" (not that a poor little three-letter word needs abbreviating), but the true name is "ampersand" . . . which is a corruption of "and per se and." However, I'm old school enough to regard abbreviations as kid stuff, a sort of unnecessary slang.

It doesn't make sense that a nation so wasteful as ours should be concerned about saving ink, yet abbrevations are a national habit by now. Maybe we are just in a hurry. But I enjoy my language and don't like to see it chopped short or chopped up. See wht. I mn.?

There are abbreviations that mystify me, like "bbl" which stands for "barrel." I wonder why they throw in an extra "b." Then the dictionary tells me that "bg." stands for bag; I can't see why they should leave out an "a" when they have to add a period anyway. Perhaps a period instead of an "a" saves time for people in the bag business? The same dictionary explains that "A" is the official abbreviation for America, argon, acre, absolute temperature, artillery, anonymous, and sixteen other words. Originally "A" was the sign of adultery in Puritan days, when it was considered indecent even to mention what we seem to make a general practice of nowadays. When they caught you at it, they burned a letter "A" on your forehead, and I guess that *was* better than burning in the whole word.

If you ask anyone what "Mr." and "Mrs." stand for they will tell you it is short for "Mister" and "Missus," but there is no such word as "missus." Mr. and Mrs. are short forms of "Master" and "Mistress." Of course you might get yourself slapped today if you call a lady "Mistress," but actually she should be flattered; it started out meaning "a woman of respect and authority." Anyway, just to practice what I preach I shall address my letters to "Master" and "Mistress" this or that, and risk the slap. And I shall spell out Connecticut because I don't live in Conn. Anyone can live in L.A. or in Philly, but only special people live in Los Angeles and Philadelphia. Actually there is a mass of people who live in Mass. who can't spell out the name of the state they come from. The Russians can live in the U.S.S.R. if they want to but I live in the United States of America. The "U.S.A." began when George M. Cohan couldn't find anything to rhyme with "America." (George's middle initial, in case you didn't know, was for Michael, and if he had not used only the M, more people would have known he was Irish and would not have misspelled his name "Cohen" instead of "Cohan.")

The U.N. building probably seems like any other skyscraper until you think of it as the United Nations Building; then it takes on its proper aura of humanitarianism and you feel obliged to take off your hat as you enter. Most churches are like that; they demand too much respect for abbreviations to be used. You never hear of the Fst. Presbtn. Church or the Scnd. Bapt. Church. But the Catholics, who wouldn't think of abbreviating Pope to PP., or referring to J. Christ, have gone whole hog on abbreviating Monsignor as Msgr. and the Saints are "St.," which, according to my dictionary, stands for street, stanza, statute, station, stratus, strait, stone (weight), stet, as well as Saint. I think that if a fellow went to the trouble of getting himself made a Saint, we might as well give him the full credit and his unabbreviated title.

Oh yes—the abbreviation for "abbreviation" is "abbrev."

from "Booz to Insulators

The bottle above and at the left is a Booz bottle that once contained a popular and cheap brand of whiskey that started out in 1840 as "Old Cabin Whiskey," manufactured by E. G. Booz. That bottle looked like a log cabin. However, Mr. E. G. Booz's name sounded so much like the early English word "bouse" or "boose"—meaning to drink excessively—that whiskey from the house of Booz became known as "booze" and an American word was born.

The original bottles are now expensive collectors' pieces and nowadays the antique shops sell copies of the old Booz bottle. They will tell you that before the day of Mr. Booz there was no such word as booze. But that is not correct, for a century before you'll find Dryden writing:

> With a long legend of romantic things,
> Which in his cups the bousy poet sings. . . .

In any case, the Booz bottle (made originally in Glassboro, New Jersey) was fashioned to look like "the house of Booz." It is perhaps the most popular item in antique American glass.

Fast becoming the second most popular curiosity in American glass is the thing on the right in the picture, which is nothing other than a glass insulator from a telephone pole. Just because they started making them from plastic a few years back, the old glass insulators have become collectors' pieces. Most antique shops have them in stock by now. Books have already been written about "antique" glass insulators—*A Guide for Insulator Collectors, The Glass Insulator in America,* et cetera. There are even newspapers and magazines that specialize in the new hobby, mostly sponsored by the American Bottle Collector's Association. Their shows feature booths that sell nothing but old bottles and glass insulators. The A.B.C.A. Annual Convention is in June each year, if you're interested. However, I gave up collecting bottles a long while ago and turned to new interests.

Originally my interest had been sparked when I saw a bottle in the shape of a fish. The dealer said it was something pretty special and I considered myself lucky to get it for only ten dollars. Then, a year later when my doctor advised me to take cod liver oil and the bottle of the stuff I bought came in the very same type of bottle, I lost interest in bottle collecting.

Recently the old urge toward glass collecting returned when I spotted a dozen rare early American champagne goblets. At my age some people begin to squander everything but time and, although the price was astronomical, I bought them. When I unpacked my treasures at home, however, I found I'd cracked one glass. That, I decided, I'd keep for my own use. In fact, if an occasion ever arose, I might make quite an impression by toasting my guests and then tossing the glass into my fireplace. (I was always a show-off.)

That occasion arrived recently when I held a small party for a friend who had just written a book. "To your book!" I cried and with a lavish flourish, I hurled the glass into the fire. My guests gasped at the extravagant exhibition but then, remembering what one is supposed to do when one's host makes such a toast, one by one all eleven of my guests threw their glasses after mine. This was a gesture I hadn't considered, and it was my turn to gasp. That has been my latest and (most likely) my last venture into the realm of glass-fancying.

Not everyone feels this way, of course, and with good reason. More than most folks think, bottles are a truer part of America than most antiques. They were the first manufactured product exported from our shores, a product of a glass furnace in Jamestown, Virginia, that started manufacturing by making glass beads to trade with the Indians. When the Pilgrims landed in Massachusetts, it is recorded that they brought with them some bottles that had been made twelve years before in America.

Bottles are one kind of antique that can still be found for the looking—in dumps and in old stone walls between fields as well as in old barns and attics. One youngster who lives near my home discovered a bottle dump in the forest, half-covered by leaves and earth. Whenever he needs a few dollars he goes to what he calls his "bank" and returns with enough to furnish the local antique shops for a month or two. "I'm not telling where my bank is," he told me. "And I'm saving the good ones for my college expenses. They'll be worth more than five times as much then, too."

Heap big Chief

I'll bet there isn't anyone less understood than the American Indian, or who has more untrue things attributed to him—like the tom-tom or Indian drum, which is simply a copy of the white man's army drum; or the custom of scalping, which started as a white man's bounty offered in New England for Indian scalps; or even the very name "Indian," which is a geographical misnomer. That old phrase "Indian giver" originated from the white man's stupidity in asking an Indian for that which he was unwilling to give and not understanding the Indian's gracious custom, which was never to embarrass askers by saying "No." After the Indian had given away what he should not have parted with, he always retrieved it and thereby received the tag of "Indian giver." I guess we long ago created our own idea of what an Indian should be and that became our image of the American Indian.

Actually the Indian is a pretty regular guy, despite his having been written about as something strange and peculiar. I remember the time when, if you held your hand over your eyes as if to shade them from the sun and peered off into the distance, you were "making like an Indian." You could get the same response by patting your hand over your mouth as you let out a long wailing whoop, presumably the war cry of the Indian.

Once upon a time, long before I became an old codger, people used to enjoy playing at being (their idea of) an Indian. At fancy dress balls there were always good assortments of Indian costumes present. Indoors, on rainy days, you could burn fancy designs into leather or pieces of wood, and the favorite subject was the Indian head. Then there were always souvenirs from summer resorts that were sold at railroad stations (remember railroads?), such as tomahawks and tom-toms and those little birch bark canoes stamped "Souvenir of Lake Hopatcong" or some other summer place. Of course, everyone had one or two pairs of beaded moccasins, and I still have a balsam-filled pillow with the head of an Indian chief on the cover that is inscribed "You're my chief concern. For you I pine and balsam."

It was an era that—in the current phrase—was corny. But Indian lore made the whole vacation scene mystic and exciting. There were Indian Lover's Leaps, and enchanting places to walk through woods and beside lakes where your ears were not buzz-bombed by outboard-motor noises—places where you could feel you were really away from the big city as you played Indian. Folks didn't call their summer homes "Joe's Rest" or "Hideaway Cottage" or "Dunrollin" as they do now. Instead, there were names like "Mohegan Lodge," "Pocomoonshine," "Minnehaha Shores," and "Camp Hiawatha." I miss the Indian theme of the summers of my youth.

When *Rosemarie* was written as a stage play, a troupe of real Indians from New Mexico came to New York, where their agent tried to sell them to the show as an authentic dance troupe. "We can't use them," the casting director said. "They're much too dull. The Broadway-type Indian is better; they give the public what it thinks an Indian should be."

Just before the turn of the century, many country lakes and ponds with drab names like "Turner's Pond" or "Green Lake" began to acquire colorful Indian names. Sometimes historical societies unearthed authentic names ("what the Indians used to call it") but sometimes imaginations ran rampant. I remember buying some land on Lake Delandpotandco, a name with a romantic legend indicating that it meant "the place where the waters laugh and the big fish jump." I liked that. But I *didn't* like it when earlier deeds told me that the place had been developed by a group called Delaney, Potter and Company and I finally realized what Delan-pot-and-co really stood for. I've been suspicious of Indian names ever since.

Perhaps the most astounding example of Indian names I know is that of the brook which flows under Route 7 a few miles from where I live in Warren, Connecticut. The Highway Commission is kept busy replacing the road sign there because it is so often stolen. The name is

NAROMIYOCHKNOWHUSUNKATANKSHUNK BROOK.

They say it was the Indian name for "water that flows from the great hills," but I'll bet some early American had his little joke in naming it.

There is one old legend in upstate New York about a chief called Buffalo who had a magnificent—but unhappy—love affair that ended in the chief and his love going to the Happy Hunting Grounds over Niagara Falls in a canoe. It was he, they say, for whom the city of Buffalo, New York, was named; but buffalo was not the Indian word for *bison* (the American buffalo), nor was it even any kind of Indian name. However, the earliest French records refer to the river area there as *beau flot* (pronounced *bo-flow*, more or less) which means "beautiful flow of water," and I am certain that the English and early Americans promptly worked that over into "buffalo."

Indian chief, indeed!

The Pitsaw.

My idea of a real vacation is to be left alone for a few weeks so I can really get some work done. That is the sort of thing that makes a new man of me. But last winter I succumbed to the advice of friends "to get away from it all" and "do" the Caribbean Islands.

"If there were some good reason for my going," I protested, "I might enjoy it. In fact, I did hear there is an island named Grenada, where they still have a few pitsaws. I happen to need one for my new museum of early American tools . . ." And that remark was my undoing for, hardly before you could say Pan-American, I was down there in Grenada looking for a pitsaw.

A friend of mine named Carl Shuster had already passed the word around before I arrived, and a lot of the natives had gathered up a lot of old rusty saws, but none was a real pitsaw. "Those," I explained, "are just long crosscut saws like we have up in New England. The *pitsaw* is about ten feet long with a curved 'tiller' on one end and a box handle on the other. One man stands on top of a deep pit dug in the ground managing the upper end of the saw while the other fellow down in the pit holds the opposite end." They all listened carefully and after thanking them for their trouble and applying to their wounded feelings the salve of a few dollars (which I later learned was about equal to three months' wages) I sent them all back to the hills with their miserable saws.

Later, one night when I was dining at the plushy Calabash Inn and was in the middle of the fish course, a hotel messenger came to my table. "There are two men outside who wish to see you," he said. "They look dangerous! They are both carrying big saws!"

By that time the saw venders had cost me a few hundred dollars in "Beewee" currency and I was eager to forget the whole idea. "Tell the men to go home, please," I told the messenger, "and thank them. Also, give them this for their trouble." But as I reached into my wallet for some bills, the messenger added, "One of the saws is longer than any I have ever seen. It is about ten feet long!"

And that is how I happened to leave Grenada the next day, taking with me from island to island, from plane to plane, through one customs office after the other, one very long, very sharp, very dirty, very rusty, rotten-looking saw. It wouldn't fit into the baggage compartments of the tiny airplane transports which are so necessary in the islands. Therefore each trip was made to the next island with the saw lying the length of the plane's floor while the other passengers nudged each other significantly or came right out with a blunt question about it. Finally I found it simplest just to say, with a lifted eyebrow, "I *always* travel with it." Then I could sit back and enjoy my flight without further explanation.

But, after arriving home with my prized saw, all these tribulations on the trip seemed worthwhile. My little museum in Kent, Connecticut, would now have its own old pitsaw. I could hardly wait to de-rust the ancient implement. The handle, to my delight, seemed to have some writing beneath the rust— probably the name of some long-gone carpenter of a pirate ship. But after some oiling and much scraping, the letters which came to light read: "Warranteed by the Stanley Works of Connecticut, U.S.A."

And that is how my vacation ended, in a spot not too far from the scene of the saw's all-too-recent manufacture.

Nowadays it may be taken as a sign of good breeding in the youngster if one hears a child say "yes" or "no" instead of "uh-huh" or "nope," or some other variation—"yeah," "yup," or "OK." Most Americans have forgotten how to say "yes" and prefer writing the strange initials O and K, which as such probably have no meaning whatever to a child, or to the average adult, either. But in case you are interested . . .

One version is that the expression began in New York, where they did not speak English in the beginning. As the Dutch ships unloaded their cargo on the Hudson River piers, the tally men would call out "Oll korrect!" as modern loaders might say "Check!" In 1840 there arose a political club to support Martin Van Buren for a second term in the White House. Van Buren was of Dutch descent, born in Old Kinderhook, New York, and he was often called by the nickname "Old Kinderhook." During the campaign, he was referred to as "O. K. Van Buren" and most people seemed to like the inference that Van Buren was "oll korrect." So the Van Buren party named their club the O.K. Club. All their banners had a big O.K. on them and the newspapers and campaign songs repeated it. That, it is said, is how the expression O.K. started, but as far as I am concerned, it is definitely N.G.

However, the expression "kid" (instead of children) definitely did begin in New York, where ships used to dock with young indentured servants from Ireland, often loaded as well with cargoes of goats. To avoid a certain tax, young white servants were marked on the ship's papers as "kids," and that is why we have been calling children young goats ever since. I remember being a bit terrified in Sunday school when the Biblical passage was read: "The leopard shall lie down with the kid." (Isa.1.6.)

A child's world today, as he lives among his elders and hears them murder the King's English (as well as the President's), must still be a very complicated, yet wondrous one. I recall that when I was a tot and my mother wanted to chat freely with the other ladies, she ushered me out. "This," I was always told, "is just a monk swimmin'." For some years I had a strange picture of a gray-robed friar who swam through the room whenever women talked woman-talk. I guess it wasn't till I outgrew knee pants that I realized that they were saying "amongst women."

The kid next door to us lived in a somewhat less conservative household, but still his mother and father were concerned about his reply when they had asked Ralph what he had learned that day in school. "I learned arithmetic," he replied. "Like one-and-one, the son of a bitch is two, two-and-two, the son of a bitch is four, three-and-three, the son of a bitch is six." The parents dashed off to the school immediately to inquire into this. But what Ralph was being taught, of course, was "one-and-one, the sum of which is two, two-and-two, the sum of which is four," and so on. The language overheard in Ralph's home hadn't helped any.

Later, when his parents went to a wedding and came home mildly tipsy from champagne, he explained to me that "drinking fornication" was usual at weddings. It took me quite a while to figure out that he'd been told that "drinking for an occasion like weddings" was permissible.

My guess is that it began with the NEA in the first term of FDR after he started the WPA and the CCC, and the IWW interfered. Or maybe it began before that with the YMCA. Anyhow, when big business got into the act with GE, RKO, IBM, CBS, IT&T, and all the other alphabetical dynasties, the ball really started rolling. There was AC and DC, AM and FM radio, TV and UHF, FIB and ICBM, not to mention Vitamins A, B, C, D, E, and so on. I long for the old days when names were rich and meaningful because they were spelled out—when people enjoyed hearing their own langauge spoken. Now we have even tired of the English alphabet, and embarked on a world of numbers.

"Give me New York City Information," I asked the local Connecticut telephone operator.

"Just dial 1-212-555-1212," she said and disconnected.

But I didn't have a pencil and pad, and my mind is such that I can't even recall the name of my second wife. So I had to look up Information again, which turned out in our telephone book to be 411. It seemed easier to make a person-to-person call and let the operator mess with all those numbers. My friend was not in, however, but he could be reached at 405-672-5656.

"All right," I said. "Call there, then." She didn't tell me that 405 is the code number for Oklahoma.

My father-in-law lives nearby, where the code number is 516; but somehow or other, I always get that mixed up with 515, which happens to be in Iowa. "Hi, pop," I used to say; and a voice at the other end would say: "Watsamatta? I'm-a no your pop!" We got to be rather good friends, though, and his name is Tony La Grotta. At least once a month I make the same mistake, so now I check on the weather in Des Moines and pass the time of day—which happens to be two hours different, in summer.

Everyone, they say, should know his own zip code, his own social security number, and his own telephone number. I don't, principally because I cannot remember 06754121220411203868282. It can cause trouble, though. I was trying hard one day to remember my zip code, repeating it over and over as I walked along the street. Therefore, when I got into an elevator and the operator asked me what floor I wanted, I said, "06754."

I miss the telephone numbers that used to have appeal because of their exchange names—like "Trafalgar," and "Stuyvesant," and "Susquehanna." I am now sixty-three years old, but I can still recall my first girl friend's telephone number because it began with the word "Algonquin" (the very name of the very hotel where we used to dine), and the numbers following the exchange name were 1924—the year we met.

"Oh, you'll get used to the new numbers," a friend told me. "Let me show you how they speed things up. I'll speak to my wife in California before you can even think of the old exchange and its numbers. It's like the speed of light!" And with that he picked up the phone and fed it a few numbers. Sure enough, it took only about ten seconds—to get a busy signal, that is. "It's my daughter," he said. And he tried again . . . and again . . . and again . . . "Why don't you send her a telegram?" I inquired. "They go with the speed of light, too." He never did complete the call and because he was unable to prove his point, I still like the old way best.

My Puritan mind insists that just about anything can be said within about five minutes unless you stutter pretty badly, and it is not decent or moral to hog the line. Children who use the phone for anything except short messages, or to report a fire or a robbery, should have their pot or LSD taken away from them for at least a week.

Recently I learned first-hand about another teen-age menace to the telephone service when I picked up two very wet hitchhikers who had intended to camp out in the forest. "You can spend the night in my guest house," I told them. "And there is a phone in the living room for you to call your parents, if you wish." They explained that their home was about two hundred miles away, but that the call wouldn't cost me a cent.

"We use the code," they explained. What was the code? They thought everybody knew about it. "We have a lot of names of imaginary people, and each name stands for a whole message like 'we are all right,' or 'we will be home tomorrow night,' or 'we are having a fine time, wish you were here.' Then we put through a person-to-person call at a certain time; we always phone on the dot of the hour. Then ma or pa or whoever answers just says Mr. Jones or Mr. Smith isn't in at present and the message has gone through completely free. Good, eh?"

"Gee, that's a great idea," I said. "And now I'm going to stop the car and let you out here. There is an empty barn there to keep the rain off, and you'll have plenty of time to think about how easy it is to cheat the telephone service. Also, you can consider that there are a few honest citizens left who enjoy kicking folks like you out into the rain."

It's true that I am a nasty old man—but I wish there were a few more like me.

G. Washington

The covered bridge near my place is known as "the bridge that George Washington walked over," but George did not live long enough ever to have seen a covered bridge; the first one in America was finished in 1806. Sometimes I wonder if George Washington was real or mythical; like Paul Bunyan, there are so many impossible stories about him—the cherry tree tale, throwing that dollar across the Rappahannock River, designing the flag with Betsy Ross, and many other stories that have lately been disproved. The popular picture of this great man, who has slept in almost every ancient house in the country, the man with red hair and wooden teeth, six foot three tall but wearing a shoe that was only a size eight, makes you wonder. As the people around here say, "If Washington could be alive today, he'd turn over in his grave."

Washington's crossing of the Delaware has been given many descriptions, but the best-known one is the painting of him with ten other men, standing up in a boat that is shorter than a canoe; the flag in the boat wasn't designed until the following year. And the picture was painted in Germany by a German artist in the nineteenth century!

Even George's birthday has been misdated; by the New Style calendar he was really born on February 11, 1732. The Old Style calendar was changed in 1752, adding eleven days, so most people presumed that Washington's birthday would be on the twenty-second of February (allowing for eleven days to be added to his original date). Yet even after the calendar had been changed and until his dying day, Washington celebrated his own birthday on the New Style calendar day of February 11 or Old Style January 31.

One recent book relates that Washington visited the same Caribbean island where Alexander Hamilton's mother lived. This, suggests the author, "explains the close relationship between Hamilton and Washington." So it is supposed to be quite possible that George Washington was father of his country, including Alexander Hamilton. What a man!

Not many know that the United States of America at one point was nearly named Washingtonia, which was offered along with other suggestions such as Fredonia, Atlantis, Appalachia, and Usona. The Southern Confederacy also received suggestions that it be called Washingtonia, "in honor of that slave-holder, Southerner and Secessionist, George Washington of Mount Vernon." That never was consummated, of course, yet thirty-two counties and a hundred and twenty-one places in America have been named for Washington.

In England when the English were still called the Angles, there was a man called Wassa, who named his farmstead "Wassington." The place later became a village and the knight who held lands there under King Henry II was "Sir William de Wassington," and that was how the name Washington was born. So the great man, if you wanted to be accurate and traditional, was really George Wassington!

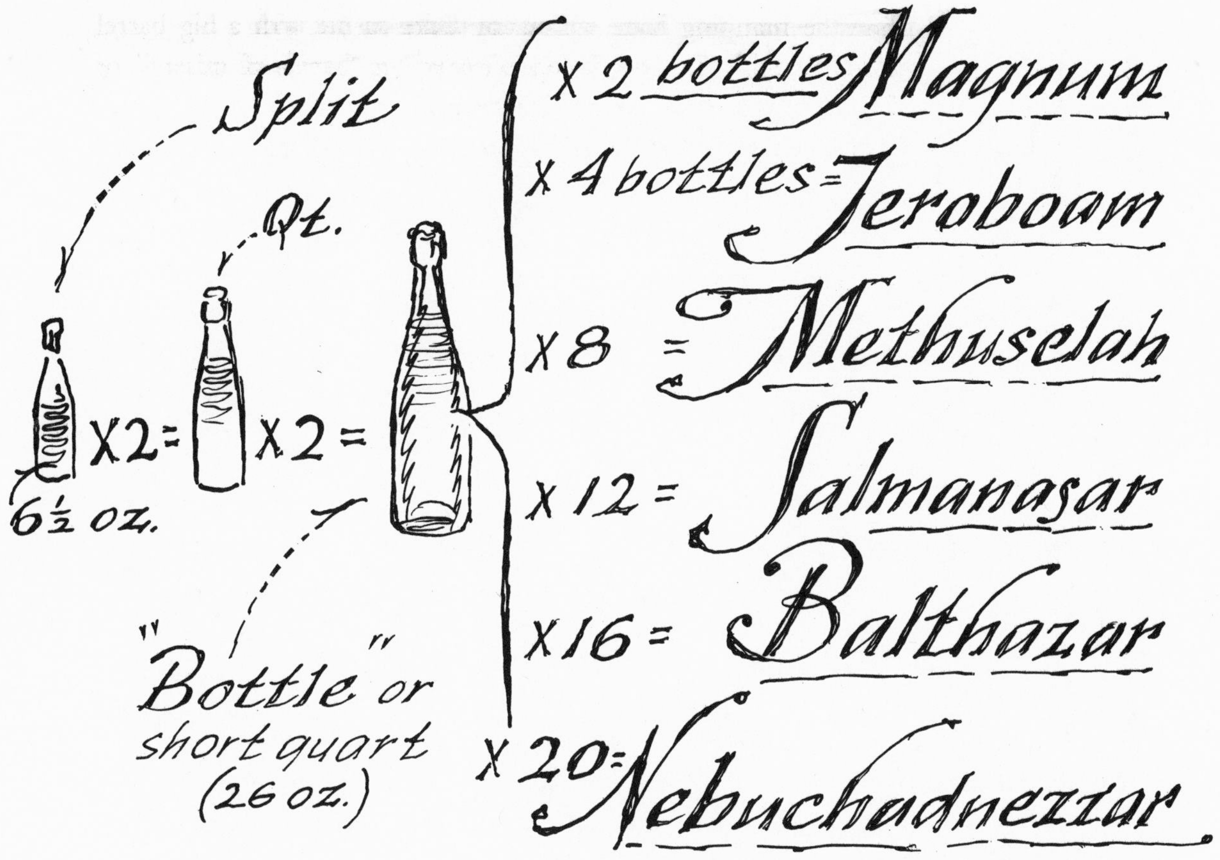

Split

Qt.

6½ oz.

X2 =   X2 =

"Bottle" or
short quart
(26 oz.)

X 2 bottles Magnum

X 4 bottles = Jeroboam

X 8 = Methuselah

X 12 = Salmanasar

X 16 = Balthazar

X 20 = Nebuchadnezzar

I remember when champagne in a regular bottle was kid stuff, and if you really wanted to impress your guests, a magnum was the usual-sized bottle. Nowadays you don't see much of the old jumbo sizes, although it is said that champagne suffers from being stored in too small a container, and is at its best in a magnum. If you are one of the old school, you'll have known already the list shown in the sketch above, starting with the split or half pint and ending in the seldom seen Nebuchadnezzar. I've never had one myself, but in the old days a whoopee room wasn't complete without a Nebuchadnezzar standing lamp or a jeroboam-based lamp. In May 1958 a five foot tall sherry bottle with a capacity of one hundred and thirty-one bottles was manufactured in England; it was called the "Adelaide," and outdid all the jumbo champagne containers. But all bottles larger than the jeroboam or double magnum have now vanished into the corpulent past.

Even barrels are disappearing. If you don't think so, try to buy a barrel and you'll most likely have to go to an antique shop to find it. The barrel era wasn't so long ago, when everything came by the barrel: that was how my father bought apples, sugar, flour, nuts, and potatoes. His attic and cellar held dozens of them, and whenever the household moved, all the dishes and small articles were wrapped in newspapers and packed in barrels. When a cartoonist depicted a fellow who'd "lost his shirt" in the market or by gambling, he always showed the man going home without any clothes on but with a big barrel around his middle. You had "barrels of money" or "barrels of misery" or "barrels of fun." Now you can't even find a barrel.

A century ago when you bought a barrel of something you weren't just buying stuff in a container; a "barrel" was also a measure. By law it contained thirty-one and a half gallons of cider or one hundred and ninety-six pounds of flour. Any farm boy knew that a barrel of cob corn would make a bushel of shelled corn. A hogshead was a giant barrel twice the size of a regular one, and by sawing a hogshead in half you'd produce two fine bathing tubs. Every farmhouse had a few of those half-hogsheads around, particularly on Saturday nights at bathtime. Two hogsheads went into a "pipe" and two pipes went into the biggest of all containers, called a "giant hogshead." The giant hogshead was often used for transporting rough tobacco, and they used to put an axle through the middle, attach it to oxen, and roll it from the fields to the wharf.

You'd think that in this land of plenty the oversized containers would be popular, but one by one they are all disappearing into vanished Americana. The smallest tubes of toothpaste are now marked "the big size" and candy bars have shrunk to about half their old size. Even the standard "two-by-four" piece of lumber is no more; you'll find a two-by-four is really only one-and-a-half inches by three-and-a-half inches. As for the American dollar, please don't even mention that.

People used to remove their trousers in polite society!

Browsing through an antique newspaper the other day, I did a double take when I read that the Duke of Wellington was turned away from a friend's door because he had refused to remove his trousers! In fact, I was astounded by such a request; but a little research turned up the information that at that time trousers were something made of canvas that men wore over knee breeches and silk stockings when they rode on horseback; they also were worn for protection by men who worked in the fields. My old dictionaries defined trousers as "long leg-coverings used by seafaring men, made for easy removal."

The word "breeches" (the sort that men used to wear in the eighteenth century) was pronounced "britches." It originated from the fact that they covered the "breech" or buttocks. The word "pants" is recent and American, according to the English Oxford Dictionary, which classifies it as: "the shortening of pantaloons to pants, which is a vulgar American abbreviation." In England today, pants means underwear. But, being a tireless researcher, reading that was enough to set me off to seek the first written use of the word "pants." I think perhaps I have found it on an old American comic valentine of 1868. It read:

> You may live without sisters and cousins and aunts,
> But a civilized man cannot live without pants.

Before that time, the old dictionaries in my collection list only "pantaloons," and that is what they are still called in most foreign countries. For example, trousers in Mexico are *pantalones* and *pantalones* mean *only* trousers. I found that out when I tried one time to buy a pair of underpants in Mexico City. My Spanish failed me. After considerable verbal face-slapping from the salesgirl, I learned that underpants are called *ropas de interior,* literally "clothes of the inside."

"While you are out buying your shorts," my wife had said, "see if you can get me some undies, too."

"My Spanish forbids such a risk," I said. "But what in hell is an undy?"

"You know," she replied, "panties."

"I wouldn't go into a store and ask anyone for either panties or undies. Or even 'hankies.' Why must women have 'tummies' and 'heinies?' Why can't they call their underpants 'shorts,' or 'drawers?' "

"You know perfectly well that women don't wear drawers! That is vulgar. If you don't want to ask for panties, ask for a pair of ladies' underpants."

That reminds me that I've often wondered why pants come in pairs? I've never seen a single pant. And how about a "pair of scissors?" Did you ever see a single scissor? You might like to know what the Sloane Research Department came up with on the subject of pants. It seems that at the time when the word came into being, you really could say "a pant." There really *were* single pants. They were used like cowboy's chaps as single leg-coverings for riding and you could buy a single "leather pant" in Arizona once upon a time. A "pair of pants" were held together by a "gee-string" just as chaps are today. And a "gee-string," if you'd like to know, was a leather string used for pulling cattle to the gee (right side) when leading them. That, of course, is how the name of the burlesque queen's G-string originated—named by the cowboys.

The first to wear the single leg coverings were the Indians of New Mexico, and when I say that they didn't wear anything between each pant, I mean they actually *didn't* wear *anything*. The Army wives said they didn't like the effect, or at any rate they did a lot of blushing. So the Army furnished the braves with a little apron to wear in front, which, of course, left the backside still exposed. That was how a famous line started that you've all heard—"Lo, the poor Indian . . ." Not many know the rest, so I might as well repeat the whole verse:

> Lo, the poor Indian whose low untutored mind
> Clothes himself before, and leaves a bare behind.

And that, dear reader, seems to be the origin of the great American pant, traced beyond our forefathers to the inventive original owners of our country.

the dubious value of being first

One of the characteristics of the modern American is the great pleasure he takes in being first in anything. If you don't think so, look at the telephone book in any big city. The New York directory, when last I looked, started with sixteen entries of places or names with unbelievable titles of "A"—just plain A. One A even had had six branch offices! Others seemed to think that the more A initials they repeated, the more this would get them in ahead of the other A initials. There was a considerable listing of double and triple As, AAAA-AAAAs and then came AAA-AAA-AAAs followed by a whole army of other remarkable combinations of A. I used to amaze guests at cocktail parties telling about this, until one fellow disagreed with me that most people want to be first.

"Take me for example," he said. "My number was once the *last* entry in the telephone book; I made up the title of 'Z.' Then I was outdone by some clown who dreamed up the title of ZZZ, and *his* number became last."

That defeat must have taken years from the poor fellow's life; but at least he was first to be last.

One of the most used volumes in my library is a book called *Famous First Facts*. It starts out alphabetically with "the first abdominal operation (without anaesthetic) in 1809" and ends its 757 pages with "first zinc produced in 1835." Somehow in reading through this very American encyclopedia, you get the picture of a lot of people who glorified being first. Some of the entries explain how others claimed to be first and even sued for their rightful honor.

At my age, the thrill of being first becomes a dubious pleasure: the obituaries are filled with fellows who went somewhere first, and I hope to be the last among my acquaintances to do a great number of things. As I think back, it is often the last of things that is the most exciting: consider the last of a game, the last of a race, the last of a banana split, or the last of a sunset. I like that thought so much, I might even do a book called *Famous Last Facts*.

People used to pen reverence in prose and song to the "last rose of summer," or "the last dance of the ball," "the last days of Pompeii," "the last of the

Mohicans," "the last laugh," and so on. But nowadays we want to know about the first of everything. Hitler's rule in war was to "get there first"! But I like better our own Walt Whitman's remark that "when liberty leaves a place, it is never the first nor even the second to go—it is always the last."

Actually it is one of life's finer arts to know how to be last, or even to want to be last. But if you'll watch the first fellow to sit down at a table and the first one to get through, you'll know what I mean about the charm and graciousness and satisfaction of being last. Or watch, while waiting for a red light to change, how most drivers want to be the first to go on the green light. There will always be one fellow who grinds the rubber from his tires and strains his gears to shoot out ahead of everyone else; he will be the one that you'll usually pass later on the open road. You will recognize him by the way his car burns oil and throws smoke from its exhaust because of so many spectacular starts.

Ye olde Picture Window

Whenever I remodel an old house, I usually include a picture window because I enjoy a good view. I believe that, if the old-timers had had indoor plumbing available, they would certainly have had bathrooms, and I think that if glass had been as available then as it now is, they would have had oversized windows too. So even though I shock the purists and dismay the antiquarians, I still regard a large window as a change nearly as necessary as the addition of a bathroom, and find constant pleasure in my panoramic views.

The very first mention of windows in America seems to have been when Edwin Winslow wrote from Plymouth in 1621: "bring paper and linseed oil for your windows." But within a few years, glass had become more plentiful than most of us realize. To be sure the panes were small at first, but glass was used as ballast in many ships that came from England, while glass furnaces were among the first industries in the colonies. One eight-pot window-glass factory, which used wood for fuel, was established at New Geneva, Pennsylvania, in 1791 by Albert Gallatin, who was later Secretary of the United States Treasury. Records show it made panes even larger than the usual 7 × 9 to 9 × 11 inches. The largest of the early panes seem to have been placed in windows of the more important or expensive houses. For instance, Jefferson's Monticello had 12 × 12-inch panes, and the Chase House in Annapolis had some as big as 11 × 18 inches. Actually the standard old-style "twelve-over-twelve" windows of the 1700s were larger than most windows in our modern houses.

What is called a picture window today, was, I believe, born during Washington's time. An example of this may be seen in the Alexander Hamilton house called The Grange, which still stands in New York City at 141st Street and Convent Avenue. Hamilton built two octagonal main rooms having wall-sized windows faced on the opposite walls by mirrors which reflected the outdoor views.

Before Washington's time, sliding casement windows were unknown and in some country houses, glassed frames were made to be wholly removed in hot weather and solid wooden panels were inserted during the coldest months. That made windows so portable that many colonial houses were sold "less glass," and when you moved from one house to another, you took your windows with you. In some places windows were taxed along with fireplaces, but one fireplace and eight windows were always tax free.

Barns and privies had no glass windows, but simple holes were cut through the walls or doors to admit light. Barns had holes in the shape of hearts, tulips, birds, or initials. The crescent cut found in some outdoor privy doors simply harks back to the days when glass was scarce or heavily taxed. And the custom of placing the temporary-looking tilted window on the gables of the house, still seen in New Hampshire barns and in some houses, began when people carried their windows with them when they moved.

The first old house that I remodeled and furnished with a big picture window has now been restored to its original small window design. I guess the new owners think they have done the right thing, but the joy of the living mural of outdoor wonders that constantly changed with the seasons is no longer theirs. Perhaps their pleasure of playing at early America makes up for their loss.

It's all in the way you look at it . . . or out of it.

the Spirit of Harvest is Gratitude

A teacher recently asked her class to draw symbols for each American holiday. The results were interesting. For Christ's birthday, almost everyone drew a Santa Claus; for America's birthday, they drew firecrackers; and for our day of Thanksgiving, a turkey.

Washington's birthday now is a national bargain-sale day, of course, and Sundays are baseball and football days.

Back when holidays were still considered holy days, people knew what they were celebrating: I came across one ancient schoolbook that had illustrated American holidays: Christmas of course showed Christ (Santa Claus hadn't yet entered the scene to take over), Independence Day featured the Liberty Bell, and the Thanksgiving symbol, believe it or not, was a haystack! That led me to do some more research. It seems that Thanksgiving was once a harvest ceremony, when farmers (and everyone was a farmer then) gave thanks for the harvest. The day the farm's haystack was finished, the Thanksgiving ceremony started.

The so-called "first Thanksgiving" of the Massachusetts colonists in 1630 had really been set aside as a day of fasting (not feasting) and had nothing to do with the harvest. It was held in midwinter, on February 22. President George Washington made the first American holiday proclamation, setting the harvest thanksgiving on November 26, with the symbol a haystack. America to this day has so rich a harvest in all ways that it seems we should have that much more to give thanks for. Perhaps we might revive the symbols of the harvest, for the spirit is ingrained in us.

I like to think that man hasn't completely changed; that the joy of harvest is inherited, that the visions of haystacks and corn shocks and the smell of newly cut grain is deeply rooted within mankind. Light a fire of autumn leaves, and even people who have not smelled such perfume previously will stop and try to remember where they knew that odor before. Perhaps in another life, perhaps in a yesterday.

I wonder if there may be an inherited love of harvest time, as if the early American reverence for the land and its crops and our ancient farming heritage might be nostalgically seeking some expression. Have you ever noticed someone riding a power grass-cutter? There seems to be a strange fascination hypnotizing the operator and giving him some kind of faraway and almost forgotten pleasure. Even if a man uses a hand mower or an old-time scythe, he will still go into that same sort of trance as he levels the grass. Surely a full-grown man looks silly sitting atop a toylike gadget and skimming around his lawn, yet he seems to get as much of a thrill as if he were piloting a spaceship.

If you should want to see a haystack now, forget it. It would be like the traditional looking for a needle in one. There are no more old-time haystacks. Since mechanized farming arrived, the art of stacking hay has been forgotten. In a day when the baler deposits Picasso-like cubes of packed hay around the field, we can regard haystacks as prime examples of vanished Americana.

Haystacks were no simple piles of cut grass. They were architecturally planned with a wooden base called a "stathel" that held floorboards that were called a "stackyard." Some had a framework built as an open cone in order to ventilate the center of the stack and this was called a "stack chimney." A good stack was usually referred to as a "rick" and it was topped by a thatched "rick roof" which was held in place by ropes. In America, where thatched roofs disappeared by the early 1800s, haystacks were then roofed or protected from the rain by a shingled gable held in place by four poles.

Harvest time on the farm and the building of a haystack was then the gayest time of the year, when the whole family pitched in to do the building, with much feasting, drinking, and music. Nowadays harvest is merely work. One man can harvest a whole field, first with a gasoline-driven cutter, then with a loud monster that picks up the cut hay, processes it, ties it, and awkwardly drops it off in squarish bundles. The laughing, the festivities, and the celebration of harvest time is something of the past; there is only work left, and no thanksgiving for nature's bounty. Why rejoice? Next year the field will probably be a housing development, anyway.

The Shave

"I'm on my way home," I told my wife on the telephone, "and I'm late. It would save time if you went on ahead to the Andersons' dinner party and I met you there. I really should get home and shave my whiskers off, but Bob will forgive me; he hates late guests."

"Why don't you get a shave on the way? Stop in at some barbershop," said Ruth.

"That's a great idea," I replied. "As a matter of fact, I can see a barbershop from the telephone booth I am phoning from. See you at the Andersons'."

A moment later I entered the barbershop, whipped off my tie, undid my collar, and sat in an empty chair. "I'm in a hurry," I announced. "All I need is a shave."

"We don't give shaves," the man said.

I looked around me. "This *is* a barbershop, isn't it?"

"Sure it's a barbershop," he replied. "But we haven't had a call for a shave since we opened six years ago. You are the first to ask for one."

"Well, I must show up at a dinner party in a few minutes," I told the man, "and I do need a shave. What would you do if you were me?"

"You can try my straight razor," he said, "and use the washbasin here." He opened a murderous-looking blade and started stropping it for me.

"I've never used one of those in my life! It's worth five dollars if you'll do it for me. What do you say?" A desperate man will say rash things, and it was strange even to my own ears to hear me offer that sum for a shave in a barbershop. The barber looked distractedly at his fellow worker. "I don't think I can do it. Do you want to give this guy a shave?"

"I'll try," he said, "but I don't want to be responsible."

He struggled with the headrest on the chair. "We've never had this thing down," he said. It seemed to be rusty. "I guess it won't go down," he decided after more struggling, "can you slouch way down instead? Just hang your legs over the footrest."

As he started stropping the razor again, I lost my courage and, asking their indulgence, I went next door to the pharmacy, where I bought a safety razor and then returned to shave at the barbershop washbasin. The scene brought home to me how times have changed. I recalled that barbershops in western America had rooms where a fellow could even get a bath. A shave cost only twenty cents and an apprentice would charge only ten, if you cared to take the risk. Now that the barber has become a male hairdresser, a haircut costs about the same as a doctor's fee for a consultation.

The word barber itself comes from the old French word *barbier,* which, in turn, came from the Latin word *barbarius,* derived from *barba,* meaning whiskers or beard, in Latin.

I remember when I was a boy, nearly all our barbers were Italians. But a century ago, nearly all were Negroes. *Chamber's Encyclopedia of New York* of 1884 says:

In the United States the business of barbering is almost exclusively in the hands of the colored population.

That explains the old-time association of the straight razor as a colored man's weapon, for long after safety razors arrived, the colored people continued to use the old-fashioned type.

It was a man named King Camp Gillette who invented the flexible, removable razor blade and started his business corporation in 1901. Twenty people paid $250 each, receiving for this sum 500 shares of stock. In 1906 the first dividend was paid, amounting to a total of $130,000. From 1906 to 1928 nearly $70,000,000 had been paid out in cash dividends. With the growing acceptance of the disposable blade, the straight razor was doomed. Maybe it was doomed in 1901 when Gillette formed his corporation. Now, nearly seventy years later, it seems the barbershop shave is doomed, too. Shall we blame safety razors or the electric razor?

C.1770

The FIRST ROCKER?

Jogging around the park, some say, is the best way for an elderly person to exercise his muscles and stimulate the heart. But the sudden jolts of jogging are not always ideal for the delicate tissues on an aging frame which hasn't been jolted for half a century or more. Of late the advisors are harking back to the rocking chair, which from the very beginning promised to be the ideal exercise machine.

When that very beginning was is not certain. In 1774 a cabinetmaker of Philadelphia made out a bill for Mrs. Mary Norris "to bottoming a rocking chair, one shilling tenpence." The chair had needed reseating, so it might have been in existence for ten or more years, or it could have been an old straight chair with the rockers added. At any rate, that bill seems to be the first mention anywhere of a rocking chair. It is well known that Benjamin Franklin owned one of the first rocking chairs, and that he experimented with making iron rockers "because wood rockers split too easily." Most authorities give him credit for having invented the rocking chair; all authorities are certain that the idea is American, possibly the only completely American invention that early.

Sitting is physical-functional, but rocking is both physical and philosophic. It is an excercise that seems to put the body and mind in harmony. When you rock, you think in a graceful series, flowing as if the mind were locked into the rhythm. When someone asks a person a question when he is rocking, he automatically stops rocking and probably asks, "What did you say?" You can rock and listen to certain music but you can't watch television and rock, too.

Just as we find today, when someone came up with a good idea, everybody tried to get into the act, and every now and then I find an example of what someone rigged up to compete with Benjamin Franklin's rocking chair. One idea was a buggy seat on springs called a jogger. It probably gave the old-timers quite a thrill, but it took up too much room in the house and wasn't worth the stubbed toes and broken legs that probably ensued. There was also the rocking bench, with a small partitioned-off place for baby . . . a sort of cradle-and-rocker in one.

Rarest of all was the bed for senile folks who were used to their rockers but couldn't sit up very well; that was simply an adult cradle. The adult cradle was usually kept in the wing over the kitchen, with a rope hanging through the kitchen ceiling: a tug on that every now and then gave old grandma some comforting motions in her bed à go-go.

Strangely enough, you can't buy a new child's cradle in America today. Of course you'll find them in antique shops, but they are used in the home for holding magazines. I don't see why magazines should be rocked and babies not, but strange things are happening nowadays. I think the rockers and cradles, the hammocks and swings of yesterday might be revived to good advantage, if only to give proper excercise to the young and the aged. When I get my first social security check, I'm going to invest in all sorts of mobile furniture. I sort of look forward to showing that life may begin at forty, but that people over sixty-five can be swingers in more ways than one.

Tobacco—
the National Weed

You hear a lot about narcotics pushers nowadays, but you seldom think of the tobacco industry and its advertising agencies as being comparably involved, yet they do the greatest job in the world of pushing habit-forming cigarettes. If you don't think so, look around you and try to find a child who doesn't smoke. Growing marijuana, using it, or even having it in your possession will get you clamped in jail very quickly; but you may grow tobacco and do anything with it you will (including selling it to babies) with no legal worries whatsoever. When marijuana is compared with nicotine or alcohol, its potential for health risk and habit-forming abuse appears to be relatively low.

Some say the tobacco industry is largely responsible for marijuana being a criminal material in America, which sounds ridiculous at first; yet I have seen the gun industry lobby against gun curbs, and the tobacco industry is bigger (and potentially more dangerous to life) than the gun business. Back in 1964, one tobacco company alone had assets of one and a half billion dollars.

Tobacco has so many paid advocates that you seldom hear from the non-smoker, so I thought that, this being a free country, I might stick my neck out and sound off. Perhaps it was when I first put a pipe in my pocket and set myself on fire that I soured on smoking. Or perhaps I found it difficult to work or eat or what have you, while smoking. I have reason to recall when I accidentally dumped my cigarette ashes into the volatile cleaning solution for my paint brushes; I still bear those scars. No matter what the reason, I consider myself lucky not to have the habit.

I find that smokers have no regard whatsoever for nonsmokers. They can't seem to entertain the thought that smoking at the dinner table might be objectionable to anyone but some kind of nut. Well, I enjoy good food, but not when accompanied by tobacco smoke; so, for many years past, I haven't had a completely enjoyable meal except those eaten alone. There are those who feel more like vomiting than eating when inhaling someone else's smoke and I am one of those.

If you ever attended a true gourmet dinner, you will know that smoking at the table is forbidden; yet the best restaurants, try as they will to serve a perfect meal, must serve it in smoke-tainted rooms. Perhaps some restaurant owner will someday reserve a special dining room for nonsmokers, but I wouldn't place a bet on that.

The argument for smoking, of course, is that it relaxes and soothes one, but tobacco relaxes only those who are hopelessly accustomed to its use. I remember hearing that the wounded soldier in World War I called for a priest or for his mother. Now he asks for a cigarette. It is said that the wounded man gets relaxation from a few puffs; but what really happens is that a wounded *tobacco addict* receives his accustomed relaxation. Should I get wounded, give me a martini with a twist of lemon.

Cigarettes are comparatively new; the first cigarette-making machine is not yet a century old. Nevertheless cigarettes have become as big an industry as wheat growing and processing and have become more the "staff of life" than bread for most people in America. Last year's production of wheat was about one and a half billion bushels; the production of tobacco was about two billion pounds. If you think tobacco isn't part of the daily American meal, try to leave out the ash tray from the place setting on any restaurant table.

One of my pet peeves is the television commercial for cigarettes that raves about "the taste" of tobacco, how "clean and refreshing" the stuff is. Well, I enjoy the clean fresh smell of a cow barn and even that of farm manure, but my stomach revolts when I must enter a room after a lot of smoking dames have had a bridge party in it. Recently after I had a dinner party and the guests had left, I decided to try some of my own salad. I was momentarily intrigued with a new ingredient someone had added which seemed more chewable than the lettuce and tomatoes. But after chewing for a while, I can tell you it wasn't either refreshing or tasty; cigarette butts taste awful, even with filters. And, what's worse, smoking leads to bad habits—like putting butts into somebody's good salad.

So there I've gone and had my say. And stepped on a lot of toes, I am sure. But as I said before, smokers have to give time to nonsmokers on their point of view. This is the American way.

Stop, look and listen!

I can remember when they used to say, "The sky's the limit." But now that we've passed the sky on our way to the moon and found that it extends only a little beyond the stratosphere, we seem to enjoy the idea of there being *no* limit to *anything*. In our habits and morals and speech as well as our speed of living, the thought of a limitless existence is suddenly regarded as the richest kind of life, the ultimate in civilization. I think there should be a limit to limitlessness. God, eternity, and the universe may be limitless, but man is not yet ready to play God, and the work of making proper boundaries and limits, it seems to me, is a fine and necessary art which man can essay.

Looking backward or marking time is out of fashion nowadays: yet just going ahead without marking time, ignoring the past, leads to nothing but a fall. Take the trend of aviation toward building faster and bigger planes, with no limits whatever considered: it often takes you longer to travel to an airport, get on the plane and get under way than the time taken by the actual air trip. The newest high-altitude planes, costing billions of dollars to research, design, and build, have been found too big, too fast, and too high-flying to be commercially usable. The first two research models to fly were worth their weight in solid gold: they broke windows and even shattered some buildings with their shock waves, and it was found that any malfunction of the pressurized cabins at 75,000 feet would not allow time for descent before all passengers would perish. Yet we are "working hard on ideas to lick these bugs" in order to keep on making faster, bigger, higher-flying planes.

Meantime I long for the old commuting trains with dining cars and clean, uncracked windows. You can take remarkable vacation-type air trips around the world, but the commuting trips which really must be made each day on trains are often hazardous, frequently disgusting, and not as efficient as they were twenty-five years ago.

For the past ten years, there has been talk about hundred-mile-an-hour trains that are going to revolutionize the American railroad industry. I'll bet not many realize that the old coal-burning steam locomotive trains of half a century ago did much better than that. Both The New York Central and Hudson Railroad and the Empire State Express were clocked through Grimesville, New York, in 1893 at 102 and 112 miles an hour respectively. The Savannah, Florida and Western Railroad's mail train passed through Screven, Florida, at 120 miles an hour back in 1901. In 1903, German railroad trains were officially clocked at 124 and 143 miles an hour, while in 1955 French trains reached 205 miles an hour. In Japan there are test records averaging 124 miles an hour and 159 peak speed on newly built trains.

In 1969, most of the railroad stations where I live in Connecticut are rotting. Some have been sold and made into gift shops or put to other peculiar uses. If you are willing to use buses and make changes, there is one antique and infrequent train which stops if you wave a handkerchief at it on Sunday night. I call it the New Haven Limited.

Another example of the modern reverence for limitlessness, in disregard of simple needs, is our highway building. The automobile, by means of streets and parking lots and highways, has started to cover the land horizontally with pavement; it is actually forcing man to confine his living to a vertically developed living space. Already in such city areas as Los Angeles, man exists on 15 percent of the land while the automobile, with trucks and other relatives, utilizes 85 percent. It seems that we might start thinking about limiting how much ground space the automobile should be entitled to squander.

Limitlessness nearly reached its peak in women's short skirts during 1968, along with a similar lack of boundaries in the schools, in the theater, in literature and government spending. But I guess there can really be no "peak" to limitlessness; it just goes on and on, doesn't it?

Buy!

Nowadays when we have everything done for us, and the individual has sacrificed his individuality, we have lost the God-given joy of choice. William Cullen Bryant was asked what was the simplest rule that might insure the happiest life: "Follow then thy own choice," he said. The whole pleasure in living comes from the continuous series of choices; even when you have to make a choice and don't make it, that in itself is a choice.

Now we are told what to do, what to buy and what not to buy. The old timer could have any color of wagon he wanted, with any sort of striping or none. When you buy your automobile today, there are only certain colors offered with associated upholstering and gadgets. You must buy whether it is to your liking or not. Any slight change would demolish the assembly line or confuse the computers.

Modern man has become so brainwashed by advertising that he no longer trusts his own judgment; instead of buying merchandise, he buys advertising. Even when you ignore Madison Avenue and buy of your own choice, often as much as half of the price you pay is for advertising. I know of one item that retails for twenty cents: the box and wrapping account for six cents of this, and the advertising about four cents, while the actual merchandise has a worth of two cents. Often times we buy things we don't really want (or sometimes even need), in packages we throw away, and thus waste more than half of what everything should cost. Those four-inch mini-skirts and skin-tight trousers that are right out of the comic book and make human beings look like fools were designed not for looks (as the advertisements claim) but to save material.

I have a friend who buys a certain bread that "builds strong bodies twelve ways," and I asked him what the twelve ways are. "Beats me," he said, "but it must be so, or they wouldn't say it." So I asked the delivery man from the bakery, but he didn't know either. Then I telephoned the main office, but the girl at the switchboard there didn't know. I couldn't reach the boss, but I heard the telephone operator mumble to someone, "There's some kind of a nut wants to know what twelve ways our bread builds kids." Actually even a chicken can't exist on most white bread. That's why I get my whole-wheat bread from a little bakery that doesn't advertise at all.

Box and wrapper advertising usually make a point of "added vitamins" but the addition is usually something specified by law because it had been ground out or cooked away by poor manufacturing. For example, I recall during the war (World War II, the one we acknowledged) when the glycerine used in tobacco curing was scarce and a substitute was found in the residue of apples. One big cigarette company *had* to use this apple residue but they made it appear as something special. "New Apple-cured Tobacco" they called it! Another instance concerns a friend of mine whose apple orchard was bombarded by a severe hail storm; the fruit looked as though it had been hit with buck-shot. But he came out on top by advertising "hail-kissed Apples." He even had a slogan, "Hail-kissed for health."

Nowadays, several brands of gasoline, or coffee, or what have you (all differently priced) really come from the same sources, and often are owned by the same parent concern. Yet the advertising will trick you into thinking that one brand is different from another. But I am old enough and sour enough (and perhaps wise enough) to think for myself. It is my devilish pleasure to choose things as I see fit; and to ignore advertising.

For example, I used to like pork sausages for breakfast although I was told they were not at all good for my health; then a radio campaign arrived on which some little brat incessantly blasted my eardrums with a cry for "more sausages." I decided to stop eating pork sausages at once and since then my health has been improved. Every time I hear a loud or rude commercial on the air, I decide that that product is exactly what I shall not buy.

There is a stretch of countryside highway on Route 7 near where I live in Connecticut that is defaced by billboards advertising national industrial products. Those are the things I shall go out of my way *not* to buy. I have found that the most advertised motion pictures are usually the poor ones that need advertising to make them salable; and by the same token, I've found the greatest pieces of art in the theater or cinema are those plays with the smallest and least sensational advertising.

It is a great game and it makes you feel like one of the human race again, not to be sold, but to make your own choices. I don't buy subscriptions to magazines, because I enjoy buying them at a newsstand; therefore my mailbox is that much less cluttered. The distasteful stuff that does get into my mailbox (where on earth *do* they get my name and address?) I return "not accepted" to the sender. It's good for the post office, good for the nation, and good for the inner self.

Do join the club!

Just before the Bang

They say that lightning never strikes in the same place twice; that is sometimes so because once it strikes, the whole darn place often disappears. But a place as solid and sound as the Empire State Building in New York doesn't disappear quickly, and if I had a dollar for every time it's been struck, I'd never need social security payments. As a matter of fact, the building isn't struck as often as it does the actual striking. Out of fifty-two strikes on the Empire State Building, fifty accounted for those in which the building sent a bolt outward and struck a cloud. As shown in the sketch above, a lofty structure emits a tree-shaped tangle of invisible overcharge during any quick change of weather and electrical charges. Clouds do the same thing. When two such overcharges of opposite potentials come close (or meet) they are joined by a lightning bolt for the purpose of exchange and equalization. The lightning flash which appears to be a one-way bang is really a series of energy flows, first one way and then the other, often amounting to forty or fifty separate exchanges.

Just for the record, the average lightning bolt is 3.5 miles long and the central section is only .5 inch in diameter, surrounded by a "corona envelope" with a diameter of about 15 inches. The temperature of a lightning bolt is an instantaneous but terrific temperature of 12,000° C. The speed of the stroke from the cloud to the ground is comparatively slow (a mere 220,000 miles an hour), while the return from the ground to the cloud, which is brighter, is faster (67,000,000 miles an hour).

People used to think that the thunder's long rumble was an echo of an explosion, but a fellow named Benjamin Franklin figured that as the explosion was very irregular and very long, the sound (which travels comparatively

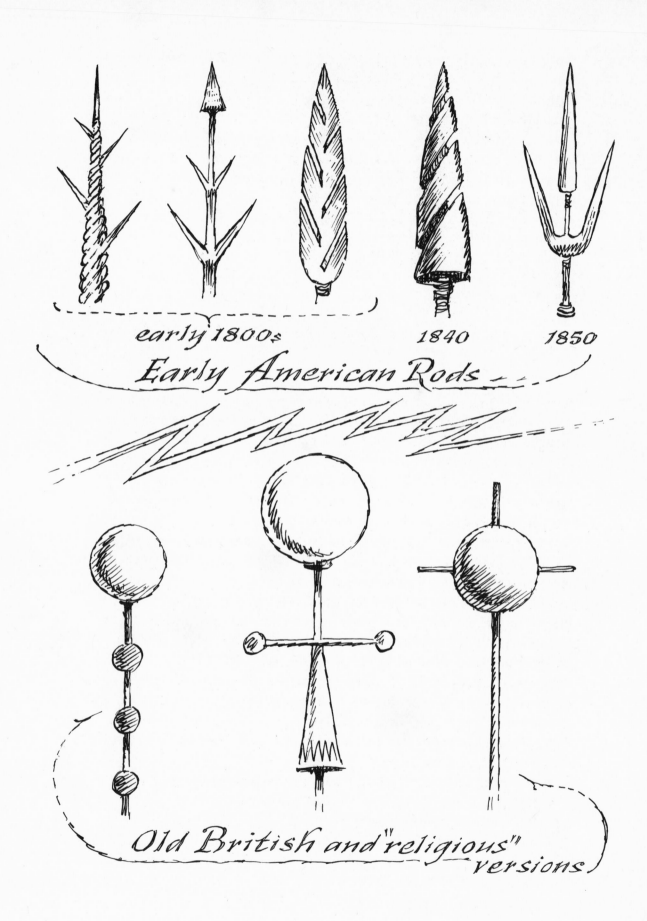

early 1800s   1840   1850

Early American Rods

Old British and "religious" versions

slowly) must also be very irregular and very long. The sound associated with a lightning bolt comes from many different distances and is therefore transformed, the one explosive bang breaking into a continuous stream of bangs of varying intensities.

All this sounds as if Sloane would be quite an expert on lightning, but the fact is that almost nobody is a lightning expert. Benjamin Franklin, who started the study, knew about as much as we know now. After more than two centuries, the kind of lightning rod which Franklin put up on his house at 141 Market Street in Philadelphia is still favored as being the best insurance. Immediately after his invention, hundreds of patents appeared, each for a different design of lightning rod; but Franklin thought the simple point was most effective.

Strangely enough, clergymen denounced the idea of "a rude point aiming at heaven and denying God's will to enforce his lightning." Ben decided this was Puritan hog-wash, and that he would sell his invention more easily in England. But King George was difficult too. "The rod might at least be polite and not offer a sharp point to Heaven; instead the rod should be topped by a round knob." And then, silly as it may sound, there ensued a dispute between Ben and the King, known as the Knobs and Points War. A lightning rod on the house that was simply pointed subjected the householder to the risk of having the windows stoned by loyal subjects of the king.

Meanwhile back in America, farmers covered their pointed lightning rods with little cupolas to avoid being branded heathens. In the big cities, things were different. Tongue-in-cheek or not, there were several patents in 1778 for hats with lightning rods on top. Both milady and her fashionable top-hatted escort had a thin wire from the rod trailing down their backs which dragged along the ground. It was all lots of fun.

To this day, lightning is as unpredictable and as mysterious as it was in Franklin's day. His lightning rod still directs a strike from the building toward the ground but nothing has yet been invented which will enable humans to avoid being struck. The fact that barns seemed to be prime targets prompted Franklin followers to wonder if either cows or masses of hay tended to accumulate an electrical charge, thus attracting lightning, an idea he intended to research before he died. This year, two hundred years later, one scientist took over Franklin's research. Dry hay, they find, certainly does accumulate electricity.

Simple things like our own earth's rain and snow, as well as lightning, are still mysteries to scientists, though since Franklin's time we've managed to reach the moon, and to make a start on the planets.

1769 ... 2069 !!

a Source of Drinking Water

My dog Spook is very annoyed with me because I have too little respect for his water fountain. It is just the correct height for a big dog like him and there seems to be an unlimited supply of water in it. But, I try to tell him, a toilet bowl is no decent place for man or beast to drink from. That is all very funny. What is not funny, however, is that your children's children's children's children will be drinking the water from all of the big city toilet bowls. Not the bowls' fresh water but their actual flushed contents! Of course, it will all have been treated and filtered. I am grateful that I live in this day and that I have my own well.

We are so accustomed to the gift of fresh water that we fail to appreciate it; we hardly consider it important. Yet infinitely more valuable than gold or anything else on earth is the stuff which comprises most of our own bodies and everything else that lives. I believe that if God were to evaluate man and condemn him for ignorance, ingratitude, and evil, it might not be for murder or all the other things we do to one another. It might be for spoiling the materials which He has given us to live with and to use.

I mused about this while hearing about the recent off-shore drilling leaks that have polluted hundreds of square miles of the ocean with oil. Although we actually have far more oil than we need at present, billions are being used for research to find new uses for oil, so that the oil industry must constantly

[75]

discover more and more oil deposits. Petroleum, they say, will soon feed cattle and make fertilizer; it will be used for a new kind of plastic; and we shall even eat it. I would rather eat naturally-grown food harvested from the land that was given us on which to grow it and not risk the eventual disappearance of clean sea water by man's selfishness and carelessness. To me, believing in God lies not so much in going to church regularly as in respecting God's gifts.

In the past few years, during the summer, we have had scattered scares about insufficient water, but when adequate rains came we promptly forgot the lesson. I wonder if perhaps we should make water a special study in our schools. Not the old conservation lessons about H_2O but a sociological study that would instill in everyone a proper reverence for water. They used to teach us in the schools that humans, to live properly, needed three quarts of water a day. They failed to impart that to fill the overall needs of the average, modern community, each person needs a hundred and fifty gallons a day. And if you count the water used in making gasoline and automobiles, electricity, foods, clothing and paints, and everything else you touch or consume, each person uses about enough water each day to fill a small swimming pool—which is a lot more than those "three quarts."

Half the water used in America is devoured by industry. The junk we throw into the town dumps each day used a good sized lake in its original manufacture. For example, to produce one automobile requires about twenty thousand gallons of water. It takes five gallons of water to make one bar of soap. Including the water you heated to cook it in, a plate of spaghetti required more water between the wheat fields and your serving plate than you could carry in one load.

Like air, you can't get rid of water; but you *can* contaminate it. There is the same amount of water on earth now as there always was. The sweat from prehistoric man is still part of the water supply from which we now drink. Water seems to be a gift that was never intended to be taken back in any way, and it seems to have been planned so that man cannot use it up. But maybe God underestimated man's potential greed and ingratitude and his ability to contaminate the earth. Water's greatest enemy is man.

A recent UNESCO report observed that one thirtieth of an ounce of oil products will render two hundred gallons of water sufficiently poisonous to kill aquatic life and almost makes it unfit for domestic uses. Yet offshore oil drilling has been advertised as "the great hope of America's future." I'll tell you a secret: water is (and always has been) the great hope of America's future. And anyone who risks contamination of it is unpatriotic, sacrilegious, and dangerous, whether he be an oil tycoon or the Secretary of the Interior.

There are plenty of forgotten civilizations beneath the deserts and buried under the sands of time that ended their days rich in gold, but without water.

Dedicated American no. 1.

When America began, everyone was a farmer. It wasn't so much a means of earning a living as it was a way of life. There was a lot of swapping involved and actual cash was not an important part of the farming picture. Loving your land and fighting for it referred to the actual dirt. Loving money is considered normal in present times, but you'd be considered some kind of nut to love dirt.

If the early Americans had lived as we do now, with such an overpowering urge to make money and still more money, there never would have been an America of the sort we treasure. Ask an average child or adult nowadays what he would do if he were presented with a million dollars; the reply is always "invest it wisely." In other words, though we were given (for nothing) what we might work a lifetime to earn, that would still not be enough—it should be the basis for making more!

If I were to add up what my garden costs, what with the plowing, the weeding, and the time invested, I guess last year's tomatoes must have cost about a dollar each; but the pleasure of a garden lies not in the earning or the saving of money; the pleasure is found in the doing. Perhaps such philosophy is rare now—but so are farmers.

I live in the heart of rural New England, yet I can count my farming friends on the fingers of one hand. At an average of a thousand each week, old barns are being torn down across the land to make way for new highways and mushrooming housing developments. Look into the remaining barns around the American countryside and you will probably find that they contain road-building equipment. It comes as a shock to realize that the American farmer is almost a thing of the past. Of course, there are businessmen operating tremendous Midwestern and Far Western farming industries, but you and I know they aren't farmers in the true sense.

The disappearance of the traditional American farmer may be a peculiar key to the great change in America that has occurred during the past century. The change marks the complete end of an agrarian economy and its associated agrarian philosophy. But this economy and philosophy is what the country was built upon, and it is startling to realize that the real America of our forebears is no more.

Washington said, "Let the merchants boast, and contemplate their profits; the success of all their schemes depends upon the lord of this lower creation, the farmer." After a century and a civil war, the farmer stepped down from being a lord to become a cartoon character known as a hayseed. And after another century, even the hayseed began disappearing. "We have now progressed from a farm economy," said Franklin Delano Roosevelt, "to a world industrial economy."

Today hundreds of thousands of farmers are being paid for the business of *not* growing crops. The science of "crop retirement" is finally recognized as an important phase in modern American "farming." Five such farms have received over a million dollars yearly for this strange service; one farm is known to have received four million. A member of the United States Senate received one hundred fifty thousand dollars for promising not to grow crops on his country plantation.

Thousands of sharecroppers and migrant farm families have recently been reported as "starving or being in a state of malnutrition" and in need of immediate Federal aid. Yet these farming people are often in this condition because of government-enforced crop retirement. The farm owner receives the pay while the workers lose their jobs and starve. George Washington wouldn't understand that. As a matter of fact, neither do I.

an American Symbol.

You'd think an advertising-minded nation like ours should have been the first to have designed a good simple national trademark. Our eagle symbol, like the old Prussian eagle, is far from being original; besides, there are more live eagles in Europe now than there are here. Benjamin Franklin was right when he said it was "a poor emblem for our nation . . . a fierce and wicked bird with very few admirable traits." He suggested using the turkey, which was completely American and which fed the first colonists and at that time roamed our country from coast to coast.

Our national flag, too, is the most complicated design imaginable: no school child could draw the American flag without using arithmetic and a ruler. The arrangement of the stars alone is beyond most people's knowledge, and the trick of making a five pointed star isn't easy either.

The first American symbol was best: it was a tree, for our original wealth was wood. Trees were displayed on our first flags and on our first coins. But I have always wondered what happened to prevent our good old American corn from being our symbol; it never reached our currency or even appeared on postage stamps so far as I know, although corn was the colonists' staff of life from the beginning. Where the Indians learned the secret of raising corn and cross breeding it is still a mystery. Corn exists only by the hand of man, and without man to plant it, corn would disappear. Its seeds grow in such quantity that when a whole ear falls to the ground, the competition for nutrients causes nearly all the seeds to either die or never grow enough to reach the reproductive stage. So, only by man's carefully planting a few seeds does corn survive.

When Corn was King

Cob handles

Corn Broom

Cob Pipe

the Corn Crib

Harvest Garlands

Corn Dolls

Knife·and·pail Corn·sheller

Cob Loom·Spool

Corn Stopper

There is something inspiring about this phenomenon that sparks the imagination and would have made it a fine emblem for this New World.

Nowadays the product of nearly all American cornfields is set aside for cattle feed, but time was when most bread meal was ground from cob-corn. The bread was rich and far more nourishing than the stuff we eat now. Columbus was the first European to eat corn bread; in 1492 he wrote:

> . . . natives were found growing a sort of grain which they call *maiz*. It is tosted, bak'd, dry'd and made into a flour.

And from those early times until the modern wheat industry managed to corner the national grain market, we had such things as corn fritters, corn cakes, corn flapjacks, corn bread, corn pudding, corn pone, and corn chowder as everyday fare. Perhaps we might sponsor a National Corn Week to revive our old tastes and these old delights.

Even corn whiskey is all-American, born in 1776. One white-oak cask of the stuff was stored in a barn in Bourbon County, Kentucky, when lightning struck it. By some rare electrical trick, the barrel was charred on the inside. Thus, America's unique Bourbon whiskey was born.

Recently a friend in England asked if I would send him some "Indian corn—those colorful ears like the ones you had hanging at the side of your fireplace last autumn. There isn't anything," he wrote, "that reminds us more of New England than that." Strangely enough, "corn" in England most often refers to wheat; in Scotland it refers to oats. The true definition of the word describes a corn as the seed of any plant: corn is just another word for kernel. Only in the United States and in Australia does the word corn generally refer to our collective cobseed or "Indian corn."

Anyhow, if I had been given the job of designing an American emblem, I think I might not have used the classical French lady called Liberty; or the ancient European war eagle; or even the stars and stripes, because they came at the end of the Revolution. I guess it would have been a toss-up between the American turkey and Indian corn. But no one would even know what I had in mind. As I said before, we don't think up appropriate symbols for ourselves.

The Troubles of being too Big

One time I bought one of those ridiculously long flashlights that the British call "show-off electric torches." And sure enough, I must have wanted to show off because on a particularly dark night I ventured out into the blackness to test my new toy. With an ordinary flashlight I would have been content to go only a few yards away from my place but with my super-duper flashlight to show the way, I walked right up to the hilltop overlooking my farm, thinking that perhaps I would see some wildlife. The light worked splendidly and I felt like Tom Swift until the bulb burned out. Too many batteries, I guess.

I seemed to have the choice only of sitting it out till morning or of scrambling back through a half-mile of underbrush; but first, I chose to sit down and think. (That's what the Scout Book says you should do.) However, the only things I could think of were variations on what a dope I was. Had it not been for my space-age super-light, I would not have been in such a fix.

Then all of a sudden I remembered that I had some old-time wooden matches with me. Within a short time I'd fashioned a torch from dry wood, lit it, and thus arrived home safely. But as I sat in the darkness it came to me how a modern convenience can lure one into a most disastrous inconvenience. I remembered how I had gone camping once with a new air mattress that sprang a leak and how another time I had taken cans of food along without remembering that a can opener was needed, too. And I recalled how the experts figure that New York, if cut off from the outside world, would last only a few days, like the dinosaurs who mired themselves by their own great weight. What a handicap bigness can be, too!

A frightening example of the handicap of being too big is the American industrial complex, which has become so enormous and so rich that it cannot afford to adopt the metric system. Back in 1927 Russia realized the importance of the metric system and it was their changing to it which helped them to get well ahead in the space program. Japan changed over in 1966. Within a short time the United States will be alone, chained to an obsolete system of measurement which was based upon the length of a bygone king's shoe (the foot) and the length of three barleycorns (the inch). We still measure land by the amount one man can plow in a day (the acre) and our cloth is sold by the distance from that same king's nose to his thumb (the yard). Perhaps all this sounds funny but it is actually very sad, and unbelievably costly. All doctors and scientists and electricians must use the metric system because it is proper, it is international, and it is also more accurate than other measurements; but American industry cannot afford to make a change. It has become so big that such a change would cost billions, paralyzing the economy. Every year we hear that people realize that eventually the change must be made, yet every year the problem of changing becomes more impossible.

Every now and then Washington selects a group of men to arrange a changeover to the metric system. Then they realize that every tool and every machine that makes these things, every screw, every bolt and nut that fastens them, would have to be junked. The simplest thing, then, seems to be a postponement.

Meanwhile, European children are taught their own system plus the American system, while the American children are led to believe the other nations will have to use our system if they want to do business with us. So far that has been true. None of us can yet tell our own height in the metric system, but don't worry; when you hide in the all-American corner you'll find lots of company there—awfully rich, but not very smart.

Art isn't always.

Every time I see one of those old-time New England spattered floors, I think of Jackson Pollock's paintings. That really doesn't worry me as much as the fact that Jackson Pollock's work reminds me of New England spattered floors. I'm just a hopeless square who still thinks a picture should be a picture and if you have to live with it for any length of time, it should be beautiful and pleasing rather than puzzling. Another square named Whistler said it better when he remarked that "as music should be the poetry of sound, so should art be the poetry of sight."

But recently when a little girl asked me to explain a Jackson Pollock work, and I decided to give it a try, a strange thing happened: I began to sell myself on what I had hitherto detested. Let me tell you what I said:

First of all, I think the camera does a great job and I don't think a painter should try to compete with it. Furthermore, an impression of something is easier to live with than the stark real thing, because an unfinished impression leaves room for the observer's imagination to fill in.

Now let's imagine your own idea of a beautiful scene, with its identical image reflected in a still pool; both the thing and its reflection will be beautiful to you. Then allow the reflection to become rippled by the wind, and the image becomes distorted, perhaps to the extent of becoming unidentifiable. The abstract impression of your beautiful scene is then merely the original made into a different pattern. So perhaps the Jackson Pollock painting is a disturbed reflection of something beautiful he had in mind.

At that point I felt rather proud of my logic and that the little girl was being taught something valuable about modern art. I felt, too, that I had taught myself something.

"Yes," said the little girl. "I see now what you mean. The pattern really does look like a disturbed reflection in a pool. But I still wish I knew what he had in mind before it got disturbed. I think I'd like that better."

I told this to my friend Victor Hammer, who owns an art gallery in New York and who understands all the different kinds of art. "Now will you tell me about modern art?" I asked.

"It reminds me of a fellow who had a shipload of herring," he said. "He sold it to his brother, and then bought it back at a profit. But the brother had more money to invest and bought the shipload of herring back again at an increased value. This went on for quite a while, until one brother wondered exactly what was making the cargo so valuable. 'Let's open a can and see what we are really dealing with,' he said. They opened a can and tasted it. 'Phooey!' said the other brother. 'I don't like it. This cargo is not for tasting—it is just for selling.' And that," explained Victor, "is a lot like some of the modern art. It isn't for looking at: it's for selling."

"But some of the strangest paintings," I said, "have been placed in the most important collections. Surely the experts know what is good and what is bad— that's what makes them expert. How can you evaluate a painting?"

Victor usually answers with a parable. "That reminds me," he said, "of a fellow who had a dog with a "For Sale" sign of a million dollars on it. 'That's foolish,' his friends told him. 'You can't sell a dog for such an amount.' But that didn't disturb the fellow. 'That's my price and I stick to it.' Then later he showed up without the dog. 'Did you sell him?' his friends asked. 'Of course,' he replied. 'But you didn't get your price, did you?' they continued. 'I most certainly did!' he stated. 'I swapped him for two cats worth half a million apiece.' And that," said Victor, "is how some art is evaluated."

After all, priceless art should be without a price, and what determines the value of any painting is a thousand things, all very unclear. I remember a twelve-foot-long mural I did when my minimum price was two thousand dollars a painting. The man I sold it to cut it into four parts, framed them, and sold each one for two thousand dollars, thereby demonstrating what deter-mined the pricing of *those* paintings.

the First Silo

One curse of being an antiquarian is that you constantly find mistakes made in modern interpretations of the early days. Recently I saw a motion picture set on a Revolutionary era farm wherein one of the redcoats hid in an old silo. That sort of exploded the story for me because I happened to know that the first silo in America was built in 1873.

The earliest silos were built of stone. They had exactly as much space underground as above it. It is hard to believe that almost all of the wooden silos so familiar to the American farm scene are products of the 1900s. America has surprisingly few original inventions, although numbering among them the rocking chair and the hot dog, but the silo is certainly another creation to add to the meager list. In Europe, the term silo referred to a "hole in the ground"; Americans were first to lift the hole above ground by surrounding it with a circular building.

There is a trend in modern architecture toward round buildings. There are now round apartment buildings, round churches, banks, stadiums, museums, stores, and airplane hangars, and critics today (forgetting that the Coliseum in Rome wasn't exactly a first in early architecture) are suddenly hailing round buildings as something completely new. The ancient round stone Shaker barn in Hancock, Massachusetts, might perhaps have started the recent trend. It was brought to national attention when a half-million dollar fund was used for restoring it. Early America, however, had many round churches and round schoolhouses, and I believe we were first to have round barns. There are still about a hundred of them left, all a century or more old, spreading across the country from Maine to the Midwest.

The most recent round barn evolved as follows: Recently a very distinguished gentleman awoke in the night, worrying about what kind of housing to build for his collection of early American automobiles. It was to be set in part of a public park and historic restoration that he had dreamed of for years. Other features were to be a windmill, gardens, and museum buildings, but the problem of choosing the proper building for all these rare automobiles was costing him sleep.

My book *An Age of Barns* happened to be on his bedside table and, turning on the light, he began skimming through its pages. When he came upon the story of the old round stone Shaker barn at Hancock, Massachusetts, built (by coincidence) for the same number of cows as he had ancient cars, he picked up the bedside phone, dialed, and wakened his architect. "I've solved the problem!" he announced. "I've got a great idea for the automobile museum building." The architect replied sleepily, "All right, Joe, I'll see you about it tomorrow; but I have thought up an idea, too. You bring your idea and I'll bring mine."

The two men met the next day and each, curiously, had a copy of *An Age of Barns* under his arm. On the spot, plans were formulated to build a replica of the Hancock Shaker barn, perhaps the costliest and most modern design of any barn in America.

"The original Hancock barn was for cows," said the architect, "so we'll have to take account of the difference between the length of a cow and the length of the longest early automobile."

Except for that amusing addition, the new round stone barn at the Heritage Plantation at Sandwich, Massachusetts, is a remarkable duplicate of the historic Shaker barn at Hancock. Who knows where the idea will spread from there? The history books explain that the old round barns were the result of an early American superstitition, the idea behind it being "to foil the devil into having no corner in which to hide." Somehow or other, even from the beginning, we have never liked to give the old timers credit for being clever, or even practical. We have always had to bring in some fancy reason for doing ordinary common-sense things.

the lost art of making your own Music . .

I remember when one of the joys of summer vacation nights on the lake was singing and playing mandolins or banjos. I haven't heard a mandolin in years. More recently, everyone played the ukelele; but they are gone, too.

It comes with some sadness that all the musical instruments of my youth are no more. This dawned upon me the other morning when I tried to do an impromptu comb-and-tissue morning serenade. It was once an everyday accomplishment, achieved by placing a piece of toilet tissue against a comb and humming through it, which resulted in the most dulcet tones imaginable. But now that modern industry has improved the old homespun paper into a soft and fluffy tissue, a fellow can't produce anything like the old music.

Once there were also canary warblers and nose flutes. There was hardly a street corner without some vendor demonstrating the canary warbler, a little white metal pipe which, with the help of a few drops of water and some human breath, sounded like a canary improvising on whatever tune you wished. The aluminum nose flute was held against the nose while being blown through by the mouth. (When their standard price of five cents soared to ten cents, I predicted America would have inflation from that moment on.) As a matter of fact, I haven't seen a jew's harp lately either. Or even a kazoo, which utilized the principle of the comb-and-tissue.

Once, when you went to the country (which doesn't exist any more) there was always some old codger (and whatever happened to codgers?) who enjoyed whittling whistles for little boys. I suppose there are still little boys, but they don't seem to look at all like they used to, and if ever I saw one tooting on a whistle, it would indeed be strange.

At one time every boy had a metal flute or two, but few of us know that the

American Indian specialized in flute playing. Usually, when we think of Indian music we think of banging on tom-toms (which were copied from the white man's military drum, incidentally), yet when the first settlers arrived here, the only Indian music was the flute and the rattle. Rattles were made from gourds and turtle shells. The early American fife of the white colonists was really designed to accompany the drum, rather than the drum accompanying the fife. I conjecture that the result was so good that the Indian gave up his flute in disgust. But the reed flute still exists among some of the Indians of the West.

The Indians, when announcing a tribal meeting, sounded an almost forgotten instrument they called a *wailos*. This was a shell on a long string which was swung around in a circle until it reached a speed that caused a loud hum. The settlers' children fashioned their own *wailos* by suspending on a string a piece of hollow wood with a long tail of paper or cloth, which they called a "bull-roarer." Every now and then some novelty company puts on the market bull-roarers made from paper, string, and a rubber band, but few know the ritual background of its eerie whine.

It might sound ridiculous to say that simple whistling is vanishing, but did you know that there used to be professional whistlers? I mean just a few years ago—not in George Washington's time. Every dance band had a member who was a good whistler, and there were several old time vaudeville acts in which a whole family entertained with trick whistling and group whistling. The old favorite musical piece *A Whistler and His Dog* was usually featured, of course.

Even back in Revolutionary days, soldiers used to whistle as they marched. Yankee Doodle began as a whistling-marching tune. Now it seems to be considered sissy or childish for American men to sing or whistle as they march, but it is still done in Europe. The thrill of hearing a whole regiment whistling the Colonel Bogie tune in the motion picture *The Bridge on the River Kwai* was as martial and spine-tingling to me as any fife-and-drum or bagpipe music.

Recently in New York, I heard a fellow walking along Park Avenue, whistling a loud tune. People stopped and turned around, and probably regarded him as a bit balmy. I must admit his whistling startled me, too, making clear to me the truth that whistling had suddenly become a strange thing and also that people no longer do it.

A few blocks further on, I came upon several young men carrying portable radios, presumably listening to pop music. That for some reason seemed less strange to me, for to find any person expressing himself musically is, I guess, becoming a rare thing. When people sing by themselves less, write poetry less, play musical instruments less, they finally end by thinking for themselves less.

A Work of Art

For a long while I've been fascinated by the tools of craftsmen. I find the hand-worn hammers, the planes, and the chisels of the ancient masters just as inspiring as the actual products formed by these tools. The designs of the great craftsmen of building are usually influenced by tradition and shaped by the work of others before them, but the implements of their trades (often hand-made) were smoothed from years of handling, a patina laid on by genius at work. Painters, however, have few implements; their brushes are soon worn out and discarded, while their palettes are frequently just slabs of old board. But they do use easels.

A few years ago, I thought I might build an exceptional easel. A man who does carpentry usually wants a good workbench and a writer wants a special desk; but the average painter puts up with the most makeshift sort of easel. Mine, I decided, would be a "dream easel." It would have a built-in radio and also controls for a record player. There would be a cabinet for equipment storage and a secure place for a teacup or a cocktail. It would be placed on swiveled wheels, there would be various kinds of lighting arrangements, and even a small electric heater for my feet was incorporated.

I often wonder what happened to my dream easel. When I gave up my New York studio I left it there. It took about a month to build it, but that easel did nothing for my work. I found myself constantly dipping my brush in my cocktail, the wheels made the contraption too mobile, and once I spilled a can of varnish into the record-player control, which ended that. Every time I executed a heavy brush stroke, the whole thing creaked and groaned like an ancient bed occupied by a restless heavyweight. The lady downstairs once knocked on her ceiling and demanded, "Will you get that woman out of your apartment at once!" I have no idea what she meant, but when I rigged up a simpler easel made from a ladder, she seemed satisfied, for I worked night after night without further complaint.

I've often wondered what happens to the easels of the great masters. Imagine the romance and value connected with the easel of Rembrandt or Rubens, or of any other great painters! I think I'd rather own their easels than some of their paintings. My own easel, which I've been using now for about three decades, is a masterpiece decorated with dried globs of paint, smears, and spills, but I wouldn't give it up for any amount. I'm sure other painters feel the same way about their well-used easels, and I wonder why instead of willing their paintings to museums they don't bequeath their easels.

Strangely enough, just as the carpenter's four-legged brace is still called a sawhorse, the easel was first known as the painter's "horse." Rembrandt's "ezel" had four legs. It was when the Dutch masters began building fine "horses" or "asses" (to hold their paintings) that the *ezel* (the Dutch word for donkey or ass) became a standard name for this piece of studio equipment. The French painters called their easels a *chevalet,* or "wooden horse." Frederick Remington, the American painter of the Old West, had a sense of humor as well as a reverence for his wooden painting horse. He called it "Old Paint."

Now as I behold my own easel with its full-inch layer of smeared paint, I find it more of a work of art than most of my paintings. Perhaps it simply means more to me than it ever would to anyone else, but I think perhaps I'll will it to some collector or other in the hope that I might start the first Museum for Artists' Easels.

ze Artiste

Artists used to do spectacular things such as cutting off their ears to send to their sweethearts, or leaving their families to hide on some South Sea island. They had attic studios and big north-light windows and they lived on bread and wine. But Picasso became a banker, and Wyeth is a quiet family man, and most great painters are impossible squares.

It seems like yesterday when all painters looked like artists, when any deluxe set of watercolors came equipped with a smock and a beret. But nowadays the average artist looks more like a plumber or a carpenter. The most successful may look like a stockbroker. Walk down the avenue and try to pick out the men of the arts: you can't do it because every bearded lad looks as if he were on his way to a fancy dress ball disguised as Van Gogh. (I was going to say Toulouse-Lautrec but I remembered in time that he always wore a collar, a tie, and a derby hat.)

Recently a friend phoned to ask if I had anything he could wear to a masquerade. "I want to look exactly like an artist," he said. "Just get a crew cut," I told him, "and wear a clean white shirt with a somber necktie."

Only two decades ago, when I moved to the country, you could spot a farmer boy at once but today they all wear tight pants, love bead necklaces, and girlish hair styles. Even the scarecrows are different now. My neighbor rigged up a Calder-type mobile that jiggles in the wind and scares away far more crows than the old stuffed-overall kind. I'm going to make a scarecrow from my old smock and beret, maybe with a palette hanging from one broomstick arm. A painter has to assert himself in some way nowadays.

I remember when I first arrived in the Connecticut countryside the residents were known to accept painters and tolerate their idiosyncrasies. But as soon as I told anyone I made my living at art, I sensed that they expected me to be a bit odd. They'd say things like, "Ah! Ze artiste!" and give me a knowing smile and a wink.

My first assignment after I settled there was to illustrate a magazine story about a dog that chased cars. "I want a shot of an automobile," the editor said, "as a dog might see it." So I went out to the highway with my sketch pad and got down on my elbows and knees to see a dog's-eye view. I didn't think my neighbors would be watching, but the telephone rang soon after I went in. "Are you all right?" they asked. "You seem to be in some sort of trouble."

Then, when I decided to close up a well near the house and cover it with a patio, I told the workmen to try first to fill it. "Throw all of the floor shavings and varnish scrapings into the well. Then burn them." Later I noticed the men running and pouring pails of water into the well. "We must have started an underground peat fire," they explained. "The fire won't go out." Finally I had to phone the fire department. "Rush over," I said. "My well is on fire!" I could hear the voice at the other end of the line whisper to someone, "It's that crazy artist who just moved into the neighborhood. He says his well is on fire." It took about a week to extinguish my well fire but it all seemed to be what folks expected of an artist.

No artist's studio was complete, according to popular conception, without a nude model or two. And an artist's party was supposed be the last word in careless abandon and debauchery. But all my painter friends are squares; they don't do any of the expected things an artist should do, and that's a letdown. It seems to me we should get together at least once a year and do something quite mad to satisfy the people around us.

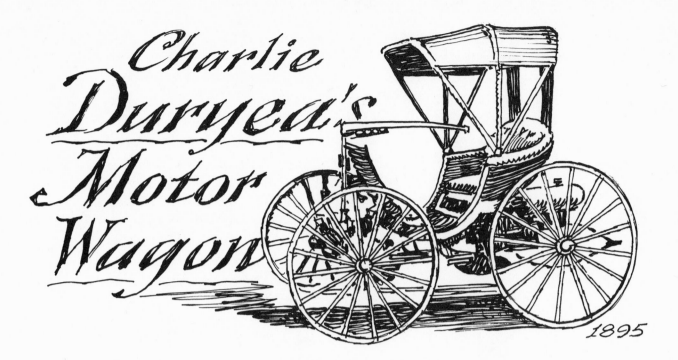

Charlie Duryea's Motor Wagon

1895

Lucky are those whose childhoods go back to the early days of this century for, among all who have inhabited the earth since the beginning of time, no others will have experienced more rapid changes. Travel by horse, for example, ended only two decades after the automobile appeared. Today's familiar traffic signal was thought of only about five decades ago, when traffic policemen were still confined to bicycles in many places. Since that time enough highways have been built in the United States to go around the earth a hundred times. Instead of the car being an accessory to man and a convenience, man's economy, his actual living space, and his cities have become an accessory and convenience to the automobile. It's been a busy automotive fifty years.

Nothing has changed civilization more quickly than the automobile. It comes as a shock to realize even the word "automobile" is less than seventy-five years old. In 1895, when the horseless carriages were being groomed for their first big American race, the owner of the Chicago *Times-Herald* decided to get publicity from the situation and offered a five-hundred-dollar prize for the best name for the new gasoline gadget. Back in 1887, when the first trials were held in France for the run from Paris to Versailles, they were won by George Bouton with a steam "quadricycle." But that name suggests a four-wheeled machine, and many of the early horseless carriages were three-wheeled. The Chicago newspaper prize was divided among three people who had sent in the name "motocycle," and the race, according to the newspaper, was going to be "a motocycle race." Other names suggested were autobat, road-wagon, autocar, gas-cycle, autovic, self-motor, gasmobile, petrocar, pneumobile, autogo, and autokinet.

The average speed of the winner was only seven and a half miles an hour, attained by Charles Duryea, who had built the "buggynaut" and then the "motor wagon." He had already registered the name of the Duryea Motor Wagon Company and he hinted that "motocycle" was too close to his registered name "motor wagon." Close enough, in fact, for a lawsuit to be started. A magazine called *Motocycle* folded at once but began publishing again under a new title. The name "motocycle" was soon forgotten. If it had not been for Charles Duryea, we might still be driving "motocycles."

More than two thousand makes of automobiles have been manufactured in the United States, and as a boy I could name and recognize over a hundred. I've driven the Apperson, Auburn, Austin, Chalmers, Chandler, Cole, Cord, Deusenberg, Dupont, Durant, Essex, Franklin, Grant, Haynes, Hudson, Hupmobile, Jordan, Kissel, LaSalle, Mercer, Oakland, Pierce-Arrow, Rickenbacker, and a lot of others that are only memories now. I can hardly believe that Packards are not still made; or that now there isn't such a thing as a running board on cars.

I can even remember the first motels. I know, because as an itinerant boy sign painter, I painted signs for the Milestone Mo-tel Corporation. I recall that hyphenation. Before that, they were called "cabin-camps" and they started in the Midwest. Each cabin had a tiny stove with a bucket of corncobs for fuel and there was a communal washroom. The standard price was one dollar a person, but you had to make your own bed.

I also remember the first roadside diners, a word taken from railroad lingo. They were all made from obsolete trolley cars, which probably explains why they still look like oversize trolley cars today, even to the curved roofs and railroad-type venilators. The first auction of trolleys in New York City advertised them as being "perfect for small roadside restaurants," and that is what they were all bought for, it seems.

It all seems like too much change for one lifetime, and between you and me, it is. In the past two decades the automobile has run out of improvements; instead of a better design each year, there has been only a different design. Perhaps someone will revive the full whitewall tire, sufficient headroom, running boards, and a car that doesn't seat you at gutter height. Recently a dog missed his aim at a fire hydrant, causing me to long for the good old days when you sat in a vehicle at a proper carriage height.

Thoughts about Banks...

Perhaps because I am in the word business and one of my small joys of life happens to be tracing the derivation of words, recently, while going over my income tax records, the word "bankrupt" kept haunting me. I thought about how the early moneylenders worked in the town square on a bench or, later, a counter. Each *banca* (the Italian word for bench) had the name and address of its owner carved into it. If the moneylender went out of business, his bench was "rup'd" (or broken) publicly and he was banished from the square. He was "banca-rup't." How times change!

In my old home town there are two interesting bank buildings. One is a tiny brick house with early American lines, simple, direct, and dignified; somehow or other it exemplifies the part that banking once played in the days when America was calmer, saner, and richer in the things that money cannot buy. This tiny cubicle sat on the other side of the Town Green, near a huge white church that towered above it. The picture created by the two was an architectural story of an era.

The other bank building is also an architectural picture of an era; it has just moved to town. "Town" doesn't mean what it used to, for towns are now centered around a shopping mart and a parking lot, which in turn is attached to the highway. This new bank, within spitting distance of traffic, even looks like the traffic because it is built in the form of a trailer. I understand that trailer banks are popular today, perhaps because they are temporary, perhaps because they can be moved easily, or perhaps because the trailer is a significant symbol of the mobile age. I'm sure that there must be some reason.

The tiny bank of yesterday fortunately was saved and moved to the grounds of the Historical Society, where I am sure it will remain long after the trailer bank has been moved or rebuilt. But if a student of national purpose should wish to understand what America is all about today, contemplation of these two examples of genre architecture would be most revealing.

The lesson, it seems to me, might involve America's reversed opinion of *temporariness*. Anything temporary, when America was young, was considered makeshift; from government down to the home, things were planned for permanence.

"Permanence and God," said Washington, "are the same." If you contemplate the ancient houses you will know they were not built for the builder as much as for his children's children's children. Building to last for more than a few years is impossible now, because in time your house will be obsolete or in the way of some sort of "progress." The opinion of debt has also been completely reversed, for in the beginning debt was another word for sin, or a trespass (the Bible's "forgive us our debts as we forgive our debtors" meant nothing connected with money).

Thomas Jefferson said that "if debt should be swelled to a formidable size . . . we shall be committed to corruption and rottenness and revolution." How right his words ring! This richest nation now has a population of people owing an average personal debt of over one thousand dollars a head, and the public debt is close to two thousand dollars a head. What the United States owes is considered unpayable; in dollar bills, it would blanket the nation, or make a pile weighing close to a million tons and reaching twenty-five-thousand miles high. If we were to pay our debts, however, we would become bankrupt; so, to survive, we must always owe more and more. Debt instead of being a small and temporary condition has become an overpowering permanent standard of economy.

I guess that's a lot of thought to be evoked by just comparing two bank buildings in town. But I'm not going to apologize for thinking. A national apology, it seems, is due for not thinking enough. Please pardon me now—I must spend the rest of the day figuring my income tax.

Look at the Sky!

I've been doing so much writing lately that I haven't had the time for reading, and that's not good. But lately some people have been telling me that my books are great, so I thought I might start by reading one of my own books. I began with my first one, and I can't say it was a real contribution to literature.

It was written way back when I was the first weatherman on TV, and I thought the sky was being neglected. I still have that conviction. Nowadays we've found adequate use for the sky—we dump airplane fuel and factory smoke and waste gases into it. But back then, before the sky was all messed up with smog and con-trails, I thought the sky and clouds were worth looking at. In fact, that's how I lost my job; the broadcasting company told me that people aren't interested in the sky, they just want to know, "Will it rain tomorrow or will it not?"

I found that city people in particular are unaware of the sky. Perhaps because they always walk with their eyes looking downward or perhaps because the tall buildings blot out the sky. "Boy, are the skies spectacular in the country!" they will say. Yet because of the prevalent hot updrafts, which make more cumulus clouds, and the dust and smoke present, which cause a deeper sunset color, city skies are usually the more spectacular. As soon as a city person travels to another place or gets to the country, he looks upward and discovers the sky.

At that time, one of my hobbies was collecting old weather diaries. It seems the farmers were most aware of the sky and its signs. The result was that they could often predict the weather as well as today's weatherman. Their method of study was to keep a ledger of the temperature, wind direction, and sky condition at sunrise, noon, sunset, and bedtime (usually 10 P.M.). There were also such remarks as: "frost insistent," "first frogs," "thrilling sunset," or "robins arrived." By comparing his last year's diary with the present one, and doing a little computing of the weather's trend, he would come up with something remarkable in the way of predictions for tomorrow's and next week's weather.

My sky book sold better in England than it did here, because the broadcasting man was right: folks here don't want to know about the science of weather as much as they want to find out if the ball game will be rained out. The Englishman, with his umbrella always ready, enjoys weather rain or shine. And the old-time American did that, too, because everyone was a farmer in those days and rain was not an ugly word. Living with the skies and knowing what they were up to was once one of the joys of living. For example, the countryman knew that:

A heavy dew at night produces a clear tomorrow, and that absence of dew is almost always followed by a long slow rain.

Leaves that curl up and show their undersides predict a shower because trees grow according to favorable prevailing winds. So, when an unfavorable wind arrives, the leaves will naturally reverse themselves.

Insects will swarm and bite more shortly before a storm, and odors will increase. (Body odors will attract flies and mosquitoes before a rain, while swamps or cellars where odors had been kept in place by the high pressure of good weather suddenly release their odors when the pressure lowers before a storm.)

During warm weather sun and moon halos will foretell a rainy spell within ten hours or so; lowering clouds do the same. Chimney smoke that curls downward instead of rising is also a sign of rain.

Ants traveling in lines predict rain, while scattering formations will indicate fair weather. The higher the clouds, the fairer the weather. The higher the birds fly (particularly during migration), the clearer will be the morrow.

Countrymen didn't learn such things from books—they just observed. Their heads were held a little higher in those days and they enjoyed the sky. Looking upward four times a day is still worth the trouble.

I recommend it.

the Fascination of Speed

The speed records of living things are difficult to establish because speed is tiring and the fastest thing is usually the first to slow down. For example, I've always contended that a man can move faster on foot than he can on ice skates. My logic for this is that forward speed depends upon traction with the ground, and a spiked running shoe placed against the ground is offered more resistance (and hence more traction) than a skate placed against ice. The man on foot will spurt faster for a few yards, but the man gliding on ice will pass him within a hundred feet or so and from there on will increase his differential. The man on skates is eventually faster, but how often do you travel on ice skates?

The fastest animal known is the cheetah, which has reached 84 miles an hour, but after running 2,000 feet his speed is only 45 miles an hour (about a mile or so an hour faster than a horse). The fastest bird is the spine-tailed swift, which has been clocked at between 171 and 200 miles an hour in straight flight. I suppose you might say the slowest bird is the hummingbird, because it can fly zero miles an hour, yet to do that trick, its wings must beat an average of 80 times a second. That is over twice as fast as an airplane propeller. The bat, which appears to be flying incredibly fast, reaches his top speed at only 32 miles an hour—10 miles an hour slower than a dog can run. Those snakes you've heard about that can catch a man must depend on a short burst of speed at probably 15 miles an hour, for their top average speed is only 7 miles an hour.

You might have wondered how fast a tennis ball travels: the fastest serve recorded left the racquet at 154 miles an hour and passed the net at 108. Table tennis balls have been estimated to have been driven as high as 60 miles an hour. The highest speed recorded for a skier was on a 62-degree slope at 109.14 miles an hour. The fastest rowing speed was 13.50 miles an hour. The fastest sport of all would seem to be jai-alai, for the ball often exceeds 160 miles an hour.

Almost any encyclopedia will tell you the fastest living thing is the deer botfly female and that it has gone 820 miles an hour. That is really the result of a misprint in an early article: recent experiments prove the highest maintainable airspeed for *any* insect is about 40 miles an hour. That is a long way from

820 miles an hour, a speed which would cause enough friction heat to destroy any insect.

I remember going through a small western town in the rain one night, observing that all the street lights were out. "It's the custom on this particular night," a man told me, "if it rains. This is the night when migrating geese go through here. They often confuse wet streets for a lake and kill themselves trying to land in it!" Then I recalled once having seen a whole flock of ducks lying dead on an airstrip at the old Roosevelt Field in Long Island after a stormy night.

Telling some friends about this, I noted their doubting expression. "That's nonsense," said Eric Ridder, an old shooting expert who knows ducks well. "If you've ever seen ducks land on water, you'll see that they land too slowly to kill themselves. They come to a near stall in the air and plop down at about ten miles an hour." I considered Eric's argument, and darned if he didn't seem to be right. But after some research, I learned that ducks land one way in daytime and another way at night. They land "full power on" at night, as an airplane might do in tricky winds. The reason is that in the dark of night there might be some hidden enemy lying in wait, and the duck wants to maintain airspeed till the very last instant to enable him to take off again quickly, if necessary. When a heavy bird settles into the water, it takes about fifteen seconds before it can gather airspeed to fly again. Should you wonder how this research on duck landings at night was accomplished, radar did the trick.

A Postscript from the bottom of the Second Barrel

There's nothing abstract about a barrel of crackers, and I've tried to write like that, with word crackers a reader can put his teeth into and chew upon at will, with the right amount of salt and flavor and homemade American country taste. I've always enjoyed researching and talking about the past: I can think of few things more exciting than rummaging through some ancient deserted attic; I guess my cracker barrel chats, attic forays and finds, are just about as rambling and motley. But as I've rambled, the thought often occurs that possibly I may give the impression of speaking from a distant past, like someone in a bygone world beckoning to my readers to "come on down." I don't like that picture.

I think maybe I am a dismal flop. I think perhaps after writing and painting for half a century, I've been misread and perhaps I've been giving a lot of people the wrong message. That startling and discouraging thought came to me when my publisher showed me the proof for an advertisement of my book. "Let's go back to the good old days with Eric Sloane!" it read. "See the past through the words and sketches of the expert on American nostalgia."

In the first place may I remind young and old that nostalgia is a disease. Like homesickness (another word for nostalgia), it is a saddening, uncomfortable mental illness which makes us sick of the present and causes an uncontrollable yearning to return to the past. If indeed I am expert on nostalgia, my lore has simply evolved from my knowledge of its dangers.

Secondly, I do have respect for age but certainly have no love for it. (The same may be said of lightning.) Age will do to you exactly what it will to a dead fish, but perhaps just a bit more slowly.

For all these years I've been trying to put over the message that great-great-grandfather was generally a better person than many people of today; not that

[103]

he was "older" or that he lived in "a better past," but that he knew his reason for living; he was usually harder working, more honest, more inspired, more patriotic; he loved the land more, he loved his family more, and he loved his God more than we do now. He lived a richer life and he was more of an individual; he had more of a say in his government and he was less influenced by "the establishment." These were the things that made it the good old times—and nothing else. These were the things I've been reaching into the past for with pen and paintbrush, retrieving them as well as I can.

But I guess people read into things what they want to. Some twenty years ago, when first I became inspired, the word "Americana" seemed to cover the message I wanted to convey. Now the word grows thin; it has been bastardized and commercialized. It has become as false as the imitation wormholes and the fake adze marks on "early American replicas." Instead of loving great-great-grandfather for what he was, we've compromised by revering his age instead.

Oliver Wendell Holmes said that "Men, like peaches and pears, grow sweet a little before they begin to decay. But age itself is no cause for veneration. An old crow doesn't sing more like a nightingale. And an old crocodile is still a menace." Emerson reminded us that "We do not start counting a man's years until he has nothing else to count." I hope that I might be quoted some day as having said: "The only value of age is that it gave time for someone to have done something worthwhile." Or perhaps I might find lettered on my tombstone, "Here lies Sloane, a complex sage, the antiquarian who hated age."

But I'm not giving up yet. I still think we can salvage some of what America started out to be. The original national purpose, the original pursuit of excellence has nearly been lost in the modern purpose—the pursuit of merely making more money. It has already changed the nation; it can destroy it. To some extent it has already damaged it.

If my readers have the idea I've been talking about an American heritage of antiques and quaint obsolescence, of covered bridges and bustles, of canal boats and "a good old past," they have not read between my lines; and, as I said, maybe I'm a flop.